ONE LIFE
MANY LESSONS

KATHY KEHOE

D1246821

I dedicate this book to my family, friends, therapists, and those in recovery who loved and supported me until I could learn to love myself.

ACKNOWLEDGMENTS

This book would not have been possible without the continuous love, support, feedback, and encouragement from three selfless, giving friends, Michele McCaffrey-Sweeney, Terri Miller, and Ann Phillips. I thank each one of you for your help, for your valuable feedback, for reading my book, and for supporting me in every way! I deeply love and cherish each of you.

Thank you, my endlessly loving and supportive husband, Bob, who is the wind beneath my wings. Thank you, Love, for all that you are and do.

In addition, I want to thank Karen Alley, my editor, for her excellent editing advice. Amy Bernabe, I could not be happier with your creative and inspiring book design suggestions. The ease of working with you is such a blessing. Thank you!

TABLE OF CONTENTS

THE
KNOWING

All my life experiences, good and bad, have touched my soul and fueled me to grow as a person. Life has severed my spirit, yet at the same time helped me soar to new heights.

I believe we are born to further each other's paths by sharing our God giving gifts. Our life experiences are our spiritual lessons. When we own our history and connect with our emotional selves, it is then that we truly unite with others and make a difference in our world. One Life ~ Many Lessons is about my personal journey and the lessons I learned along the way. My losses, traumas, joys, and challenges contributed to who I am today. In sharing some of my experiences, my hope is to help you heal, soar, and share your unique gifts with others.

I was four years old when "The Knowing" visited me. It was early morning, and I was standing in our front yard beneath a pear tree. I watched my neighbor, Mr. Driscoll, walk down the side steps of his house and place his lunch in his car. He returned to his house and retrieved the trash and put it into a backyard bin. Afterward, he got in his car and drove off to work.

I sat beneath that pear tree in our yard, looking to the heavens, and thought to myself, "There has got to be more to life than getting up and going to work every day. But what is it?" At that precise moment, I knew my life would be difficult. I did not know how or why, but I clearly understood that my childhood experiences would be used to help others in my future. I knew my suffering would not be in vain. I was sure the God within me would see me through it all. I also knew that no one could take from me what remains the most essential part of my life, my "inner divinity."

How does a four-year-old comprehend such things? I'm not exactly sure. But at that time I understood my experiences would serve a greater purpose and that more information would be provided when I was ready to receive it. I accepted my fate. My early life would be harrowing, but God would see me through. God is within every one of us, and ready to guide us if we but seek him.

There have been many times in my life when I intentionally ignored God. I refused to pray because I was too hurt, angry, and resentful. I struggled. Life was challenging to say the least. Yet, somehow, I always found my way back to God. God was who I trusted and leaned on because people frightened me. God remains my lifeline today.

I remain amazed by my wise, four-year-old soul as I scan through my memories. How does a child understand matters of divinity? I believe it is because wisdom comes from within. Messages come to us when we are ready to listen. We house a pure, spiritual knowing within. The spark of God lives within us, ready to guide us at any time, and one of my times was in my early childhood.

In sharing my experiences and some of the lessons learned, I hope to help you to understand that all life experiences matter, and propel us all to create more authentic and meaningful lives.

CHAPTER 1

THE
BEGINNING

*"Hurt children, wounds unhealed, too
often become very dangerous adults."
–Marianne Williamson*

I am a twin to my brother Bozie. I have a few family pictures of us together in a playpen on our First Holy Communion, and we were decked out in fancy clothes. I also have a couple of our school pictures. The photos capture happy moments in time, memories I faintly recall. As I grew older, I could look at those pictures and also detect pain and sadness in my eyes.

If my childhood had a theme, it would be, "Please don't kill me." It sounds dramatic, but unfortunately it is true. I was terrified of the unpredictable domestic violence and alcoholism that overshadowed my childhood. Horrible experiences embed themselves into the cells of my being.

As an adult, I came to understand that our physical bodies house our histories. Carrying around unresolved emotional baggage from the past wreaks havoc on ourselves and others. If we fail to deal with our emotions and issues, there is little room for joy and happiness. It took me years before I was willing and able to deal with my emotions and childhood issues.

I remember happy times as a child. We went on family car rides, ate ice cream cones, and skipped to the corner store for penny candy. We learned to appreciate what nature and animals had to offer. My childhood wasn't all bad, but the negative experiences overshadowed the good times.

Domestic violence is horrific for children. Violence creates trauma and terror within us. That was certainly true for me. I learned the danger signs well, even as a young child. Days when I came home from school to find my mother drinking while she was cooking dinner, I knew it would undoubtedly be a stormy night.

As insane as the chaos and crazy times were, my siblings and I always had meals, a warm bed, clothes, and much of what we physically needed to survive. I felt loved. I was taught to be grateful because others had much less than we did. We often gave to those in need. My mother was a very strong, empathetic, and spiritual woman. She had an unshakeable belief in a loving and forgiving God. I grew up believing we were beyond blessed in many ways.

Pain, regardless of where it originates or whether it is emotional, mental, physical, or spiritual, feels similar to each of us. In my case, my father was a very broken, sick man who deeply hurt me, my siblings, my mother, and others. The things he did caused scars in us. No one could ever deny the traumatic impact of his actions.

Because of my history, I can easily detect the pain, anguish, and scarring within others. The greater the pain, the greater its impact on our lives. I also can see how others frequently minimize and justify the impact of their experiences because they compare their lives to others who, in their judgment, endured worse. Minimizing our experiences and comparing ourselves to others is frequently an excuse to avoid dealing with our own painful pasts.

It takes great courage to acknowledge our pain and understand its causes. It takes even greater insight to own the pain we have caused ourselves. We must be brutally honest with ourselves, regardless of where we have been or what we have experienced. We must look at all aspects of our past and how it impacts our present. We are bound to the past when we minimize and deny our histories. We do our best at any given time, but sometimes our best is not enough. The unresolved brokenness in all of us impacts every aspect of our present and future.

My hope is that by sharing pieces of my story, others will be able to see and understand their own pain, find ways to deal with it, and create healthier lives. Just because your story may not be as traumatic as someone else doesn't mean your pain isn't real. It is only through facing our inner struggles and emotions that we will be able to truly move on in life.

CHAPTER 2

SURVIVAL

*"If we stop distracting,
we will stop destroying."
– Jeff Brown*

Living is very different than surviving. Trying to live and maintain some semblance of sanity amid heart-wrenching life circumstances is extremely difficult. Many of us have witnessed or experienced unimaginable human acts of evil. Pain and trauma change us in so many ways, often leaving invisible, emotional scars. Studies have shown how trauma changes our brain chemistry. In survival mode, there is no time to process emotions. Instead, we robotically act without feeling the feelings of the events. During such times, our histories and emotions store themselves into the cells of our bodies. Unresolved emotions accumulate over time. Eventually, we frequently overreact at the littlest of issues because a current event triggers the mountain of repressed emotions. That is likely when we explode, releasing our emotions, and often hurting those we love, including ourselves, in the process.

I remember being at my friend's house, hanging out with her and her older sisters, when I was about eleven years old. We were kids. Their neighbor, an older guy, purchased liquor for us underaged kids. I clearly remember drinking my first tumbler of clear alcohol, maybe gin or vodka. I grimaced, nearly puking, at the taste of it. Yet, I swallowed every drop. I was desperate to escape my reality as I did not know how to deal with the overwhelming and terrifying emotions within me. I often drank until I fell asleep. I was trying to survive and excessive alcohol enabled me to do so.

At 12 years old, I began experimenting with various other drugs, which further enhanced my ability to escape. I felt depressed and desperate when sober.

Alcohol and substances were my escapes. It would be near a decade later, that I realized my life was out of control. During those years, I lost friends, cousins, my twin brother, and more.

Drugs and alcohol enabled me to repress a mountain of unresolved pain and trauma. I was unequipped to deal with life. I had minimal coping skills, and often lacked the desire to live. Thoughts of dying offered a bit of mental and emotional relief. The only thing that kept me from suicide was the fear of death. I questioned death and wondered if it could be worse than what I was experiencing. Somewhere deep within, I had a fleeting sliver of faith and hope that things could get better. I hung on and today, truly believe I am a miracle. I believe God did for me what I could not do for myself.

As I reflect on my past, I can easily understand how I went down that path of destruction. I was in a dark alley, making even darker decisions. It was the best I could do at that time. I do not blame myself or others. It was how I survived. I was afraid to live, yet too scared to die.

Today I have great empathy and compassion for the young girl I was and all I overcame. It was a lot. I did the best I could have at that time, like most of us do. So many people experience significant pain, suffering, and anguish in their lives. I know I am not alone. What I learned from that time in my life is how to survive. I am beyond blessed to be alive and to share pieces of my story because so many did not survived a similar path.

There comes the point in life when we become sick and tired of suffering. When we suffer enough, we become willing to try to find another way. We must take full responsibility for where we have been, where we are today, and where we want to go. Nobody can do that for us. Living and surviving are choices. We have the power to change our lives as to how we want to proceed. It's a conscious choice.

When that time came for me, a short, sweet prayer helped me to begin changing my life. I had no answers. I was so sick and tired of my past, present, and where I was going. In desperation, I asked God to please help me. "Please help me to stop suffering. Please, God, help me to love me as you do."

There were times, I wasn't sure I believed God could or would help me. I was desperate, lost, and dying emotionally, mentally, physically, and spiritually. I called out to God in anguish. In time, my thoughts and decisions improved. I sought help through counseling and reconnected with my spirituality. I ceased using drugs. I found other ways to escape. I no longer drank until I passed out, but just enough to keep my emotions at bay. I engaged in other addictions such as work, food, nicotine, and exercise became new avenues to escape my emotions and memories.

Nearly a decade later, at age 31, a therapist challenged me to stop drinking. She said I had a problem with alcohol. I bet her I could and I attended my first 12-Step meeting. It was when I became totally sober that my internal wounds, memories, and emotions exploded into my consciousness. I also began to realize and accept that I was an alcoholic.

Life is complicated and trying at times for most

of us. We are exposed to life's challenges in a myriad of ways. What is important is how we face those challenges. Our difficulties or tragedies can fuel us to grow mentally, emotionally, and spiritually. We can become more, despite pain and suffering. Sometimes bad things happen in life. I know beyond a shadow of a doubt that within us, we possess the tools to deal with whatever comes our way. Despite difficulties, we can become stronger, healthier, and more resilient. How we choose to deal with life circumstances makes or breaks us.

Pain leaves indelible scars. Yet, all scars fade in time. Our wounds do not define us. When we trust in a power greater than ourselves to help us heal and grow, we can become more than we ever dreamed. Resisting emotions and allowing them to build up within us increases the duration of our pain and suffering. Accepting and embracing how we survived is the beginning. Treating ourselves with tenderness and love for what we've endured is essential. Repressed emotions prevent us from fully living. The more we distract and repress, the greater the challenge we face. Pain does not last forever. Pain leaves invisible scars. However, our scars build character that enables us to create the lives we deserve and to fulfill our greater purpose.

CHAPTER 3

LIFE PURPOSE

"Our tragedies are our academies."
– Lt. Dave Grossman

Everyone has a sacred life purpose, that helps to enhance the greater universe. We must heed our inner, divine wisdom to fulfill our purpose. Listening to others more than we do to ourselves leads us further and further away from our paths. Our answers are within. It's in the silence of being with ourselves that we begin to understand all of who we are and what our purpose is here on earth. Tuning into the divine whispers within is a learned skill that takes time and practice. The more we do it, the better we become at fulfilling our destinies.

The massive technological world we live in today makes it beyond easy to escape ourselves. Phones, watches, computers, TV, games, and so much more create noise and chaos, making it near impossible to hear our inner wisdom. Quickly we get lost in the shuffle of a busy lives and grow further and further away from ourselves.

In my life, the seedlings of my purpose began to sprout through the difficulties I experienced. Unfortunately, negative experiences seem to permeate our beings and often linger longer than positive ones. Why is it that criticism stays longer than a compliment? We cannot always control what happens in life, but we always possess the power to become more, despite it. Beneath our painful life experiences are beautiful spiritual lessons.

My life purpose sprouted shortly after the sudden death of my 18-year-old twin brother. His name was Peter, but we all called him Bozie. I found Bozie dead on June 23, 1974, at my high school graduation party held at our family home. Bozie didn't graduate the same day as me. He had a learning disability and unresolved emotional issues, and had transferred to a different school years before. He attended a vocational tech school and would have graduated later that year.

Many factors fed into his educational and emotional issues. The lack of understanding of learning challenges at that time and our Catholic School's shaming disciplinary tactics exacerbated his issues. Midway through third grade, he transferred to a school for those with special needs. His departure was painful for both of us. My brother was a sensitive soul and hurt easily. Life proved too much for him to handle. I sometimes wonder how sad he must have felt that day because we always thought we would graduate together.

I was inside our house talking with my boyfriend Jack at the party. Suddenly, my 17-year-old cousin Beverly came and said something was wrong with Bozie. Jack and I quickly followed her into the front yard. I had seen my brother minutes earlier, and he was fine. He smiled as he walked past me. A charming, sweet, crooked, and heartwarming smile touched my heart and soul.

Bozie was in his van, the 1970-something party bus where he and several of his friends were sitting in drinking pony beers. Peering inside the truck, I saw my brother's six-foot frame seated against the side wall of his van with his long legs stretched out in front of him. His head was leaning to the side, and he appeared to be sleeping. His long, wavy, light-brown hair hung partially in his eyes. I gently shook his foot, calling his name to arouse him. His head rolled softly from side to side, but there was no response. My heart began racing. "Help me get him out," Jack yelled to my brothers' friends, quickly taking control of the situation. We pulled him out and leancd his lanky body against the fence post. While we held him upright against the fencepost, Jack started CPR and told me to push on my brother's abdomen. After a few minutes with no response, Jack said we had to get him to the hospital. Quickly, Jack, myself, and a few of my brother's friends carried Bozie to Jack's car and placed him in the back seat.

There was no time to go to the house to tell the rest of the family what was happening. Off we sped to the emergency room several miles away. I remember turning around and looking at my twin brother in the back seat. His upper body leaning against the backseat door. In that moment, I realized my brother was gone. My heart sank in disbelief. Just thirteen days earlier, we celebrated our eighteenth birthday. Not long after arriving at the hospital, a doctor confirmed my brother death. He asked if I wanted to say goodbye. I did. My insides exploded in horrific disbelief.

The year following my brother's death remains a complete blur. I was beyond grief stricken and so unequipped to deal with life. I started college as planned after graduation, but dropped out after a few semesters. I had too much inner pain and turmoil to concentrate. The pressure of college proved too much at that time.

For the next four years, I escaped into drugs and alcohol to numb my pain. I was 22 years old, had worked multiple jobs but was very despondent and lost. One night, while watching a religious program with my mother, I prayed with the TV host and became a born-again Christian. It was a very powerful spiritual awakening. My mother was elated because she had been asking God to help me find my way. My spiritual experience was very energizing and up-lifting. I immediately ceased abusing drugs, returned to our community college, and completed the remaining courses and obtained my Associates Degree in Human Development. I went on to a four-year college and received a dual Bachelor's Degree in Elementary and Special Education in 1981.

Looking back, it's not surprising I began working with children and adults with special needs. No doubt, my unconscious issues were playing out. It would still be years before I connected the dots between my career interests and my childhood experiences. Was I trying to help others escape Bozie's fate? Perhaps. Regardless, it was the beginning of living my life purpose.

I obtained my teaching degree and worked in the schools dealing with children with academic and emotional needs. After three years of working in the schools, I began to resent the academic work, but I loved working with those with emotional issues. I moved to Tennessee, following a brief visit to see a boyfriend, and wound up living there for the next ten years. My then boyfriend left to travel the country and I stayed behind. Tennessee was where I entered a rehab on June 6th, 1988, and I have maintained my sobriety until this day. Shortly thereafter, I entered graduate school and received my Master's Degree in 1992.

After obtaining my master's degree in social work,

I completed the requirements to become a Licensed Clinical Social Worker. My work focused on helping those who endured emotional, physical, and sexual trauma. I was also interested in and began working with death and dying, which I continued to do for decades. I always maintained a private practice aside from my hospice work, and loved to help others create lives they love. I began to connect the dots and began to understand how my early life experiences influenced my career choices. For many years, thereafter, I continued to process my painful past.

I've noticed similar paths with others. One friend, Michele, rarely had a voice in her family because her two other siblings demanded more time and attention from her parents. She was often silenced and her needs and wants were seemingly overshadowed by those of her siblings. She realized at a young age that speaking up wasn't worth the reaction from her family, so she remained silent, repressing her feelings. Michele went on to became an exceptional teacher/advocate/mentor to many children and adults in her career. She ensured that every child she encountered was heard and knew they had self-worth.

Another friend, Terri, grew up longing to be involved in recreational programs but was only minimally permitted to as a child. She became a successful recreational director. She remains committed to ensuring all children, including those with differences, have access to and can participate in fun, exciting recreation programs. Her programs focus on enhancing children's growth and providing them great joy, laughter, and a strong sense of belonging.

Life purposes sprout in so many ways. There's no one way to get there. Finding and living your life purpose is a process. It is not an event. Our gifts and purposes are our responsibility to uncover. Our divine gifts are designed to help others further their spiritual paths.

Sometimes we find our passion and purpose by eliminating the things we find we do not like or do not want to do. That realization always brings us closer to what we are supposed to do. Our purposes are frequently connected to our passions. What I know for sure is that when we discover our gifts and purpose, a deep knowing resonates within our souls. There is no more guessing. It is clear that this is what we are here to do.

I am truly grateful for my experiences because they contributed to my character and taught me so much. The difficulties in my life helped put into perspective what was truly important. My life is meaningful and purposeful thanks to the challenges I faced. My history taught me that healing is possible. Silver linings can be found in the worst of situations. Priorities become clearer.

Being fully present with ourselves and listening to our divine, inner wisdom takes time, practice, and commitment. To accomplish this we must tune out the outside voices or influences is necessary. Our path is ours and no one else's. Sit in silence and hear your inner wisdom. It's there. Living on purpose and with purpose offers us greater joy, satisfaction, and passion and fuels us to become more.

We are equal in God's eyes. No one person is more worthy than another. We are capable of great things. We can choose to live or to merely exist. We can follow our inner wisdom, or we can do and be what others tell us to be. We can float through life without direction or decide to live with intention. It's our choice. Let's own our gifts and soar into all of who we are. Our gifts and purposes are needed, wanted, and vital to the universal whole. Our divine gifts assist others along their way. We can and must do our part to discover our unique life purposes. It's our responsibility to ourselves and each other.

CHAPTER 4

FEAR
VERSUS FAITH

*"Faith and fear both demand you believe in
something you cannot see. You choose."*
— Bob Proctor

Fear dominated much of my childhood. The unpredictability of domestic violence created a steady dose of fear coursing through my body daily. Fear can easily be triggered in me even today. Anxiety is often debilitating and paralyzing. Fear prevents us from growing. It impedes our ability to connect with God or a higher power. Yet, we always have a choice as to whether or not we want to entertain fearful thoughts and the harmful impact of them on our lives. We cannot control the thoughts that float into our heads, but we have the power to change our thoughts. We do not need to obsess about the what-ifs fear often triggers. We do not need to obsess about the what-ifs that fear often triggers.

Fear has negatively impacted my thinking, decisions, relationships, and life despite my faith. As an adult, I learned to appreciate fear for what it has to teach me. Fear protects us and keeps us safe, but it also prevents us from becoming all we are born to be. It's a powerful emotion that warrants examination. Do we allow fear to stop us from becoming more, or do we walk through it? The choice is ours.

Fear can also manifest into other emotions such as anxiety, anger, and defensiveness if repressed. Eleanor Roosevelt said, "You gain strength and confidence by every experience in which you stop to look fear in the face. You must do the thing you think you cannot do." Walking through our fears opens the door to greater possibilities and opportunities in our lives. Living in fear impedes our growth and keeps us stuck in place.

A few years ago, I was diagnosed with Stage IV lung

cancer, inoperable and terminal. The level of fear I felt at that time was profound. I couldn't sleep, eat, or think clearly. Fear caused me to replay my mother's death from lung cancer and the many difficult hospice deaths I witnessed in my career. I was beside myself with a thousand what-ifs. I quickly realized that I would surely die if I continued down that gut-wrenching, fearful path. I knew I had to change my thoughts about cancer and dying if I desired to live.

I suffered and struggled mentally and emotionally for a while. However, waiting to die is not living. It's barely surviving. If I didn't change my thinking and my attitude, the rest of my life would be sad, depressing, and negative. I had to fight and find a way to live, despite cancer.

I prayed to God's for the help I needed to act my way into better thinking. I began to work diligently doing what I could to help myself mentally, emotionally, physically, and spiritually. I connected with positive and hopeful lung cancer survivors who were fully and beautifully living their lives. Some of those survivors were initially much worse off than me, yet they continued to live a good quality of life. Those survivors are my idols.

I learned that cancer is only a six-letter word. It is a very powerful word. I knew the cancer inside of me was only a tiny part of who I am. It is not all of me. Cancer teaches me to pay close attention to how I live my life, to evaluate all my relationships, to determine what brings me joy, and to closely examine my thoughts and emotions. I focus on what cancer teaches me rather than what it costs me. I focus on living, as opposed to dying. I realize that death will visit all of us, but I want to live the rest of my life well. Cancer propels me to do only what I love, with only those I desire to be with, and to be ever grateful. I had to let go of toxic people, situations, and places. I surrounded myself with those who love me well and are positive and appreciative. Cancer taught me to truly honor my time and live each day as if it is my last.

Shortly after my diagnosis, I recall a mentor telling me how grateful she was to have cancer, and I thought to myself, she is crazy. Yet, the longer I live with cancer, the more I understand the depth of what she meant. The quality of my life is so much better than before my diagnosis. Cancer taught me to take great care of myself. I value life, and every day I wake up to a new world of possibilities and opportunities to serve.

There are times when fear rears its head, especially when I have aches, pains, lethargy, scans, tests, treatments, and more. I remind myself that I am in control of my thoughts and actions, and I have choices. Living in fear drains and stagnates me. I focus on life and doing what I am passionate about, and connecting with loving others. Life is a gift. We can choose to live fully, intentionally, and freely. Fear imprisons us in a sea of despair and negativity. We must want more than that for ourselves. We can soar despite cancer!

How can we walk through and beyond our fears? First and foremost, we must decide to do so. We can use fear to propel us through it. We either entertain our worries, or we change our stinking thinking. When fearful thoughts float into our consciousness, we replace them with positive, hopeful thoughts. For example, it is easy to think "I have cancer, I am going to die!" We can always change our mindset with thoughts such as, "Yes, we have cancer, but it is only a tiny part of us. We are so much more than this cancer."

I also ask myself, what lesson am I to learn from this cancer? Our struggles are often spiritual lessons to teach us to become more. We must pay attention. We cannot allow fear to control our lives. We must change and correct the crazy, involuntary thoughts that rob us of living well.

The more we focus on fearful thoughts, the more immobilized we become. Once immobilized, our fear blocks us from seeing alternative options. With consistent effort, we can act our way into better thinking. We may have to fake it until we make it. Walking straight through our fears is possible and necessary to create the lives we love.

Marianne Williamson wrote that "We are afraid of our brilliance." It's so true. Many of us are afraid of all we can become. We hide behind humility, what others will think or respond, and so much more. It is not necessary. We are supposed to allow our light to shine brightly in the world. Our gifts are meant to be shared to assist others in furthering their paths.

It is essential to pay attention to those we surround ourselves with. So many people live in fear. Their fear often unconsciously fuels ours. Pay attention to those who support us, encourage us, and fuel us to become all we can be. They are the positive cheerleaders we need to walk with us through our fears. We must also recognize those who are too fearful to examine their own lives. Undoubtedly, some of these people may be our parents, children, spouses, friends, etc. Negative and fearful people drain our energy, and that is dangerous. To truly live our lives, we must reserve energy for ourselves. We cannot soar if we allow others to drain us and rain on our parade. We cannot blame them if we willing give away our power.

For too many years, I've focused unnecessary energy on trying to understand toxic people and their behavior. I erroneously thought that I would feel safer if I could just figure out why they acted in such harmful ways. After decades of spinning my wheels, I've realized I wasted so much valuable time focusing on those who hurt me, rather than those who love me. I wasted my precious time on others who did not deserve my time and attention. I learned the importance of having great faith in myself and to honor the relationships that foster my growth. Life became more joyful, fun, and positive when I cut out draining people.

Having faith in something or someone greater than ourselves is necessary at times. Faith transcends fear. Asking a higher power to dissolve our fears and enable us to see what we must see and to do what we must do. Sometimes, asking God to do for me the things I cannot do for myself is needed. We often need to get out of our own way and cease sabotaging our hopes and dreams. If what we are doing is not working, then perhaps it's time to let go and let God or whatever we believe in to assist us. What have we got to lose?

CHAPTER 5

FORGIVENESS
LIBERATES US

"Forgive others, not because they deserve
forgiveness, but because you deserve peace."
– Mel Robbins

Forgiveness is a complicated and often misunderstood word. Webster's dictionary defines the word forgive as "To give up resentment of or requital. To pardon or absolve." Forgiveness triggers great emotion and has a powerful impact on our lives, whether we realize it or not. The lack of forgiveness forever bonds us to painful people and experiences.

Let's examine what forgiveness is not. Forgiveness is not mean condoning hurtful people or behavior. We need not pardon the offender or continue a relationship with them. However, until we forgive them or their actions, we remain energetically tied to them. Forgiveness is not something we do for the sake of others. It is a gift we give ourselves.

What is forgiveness?
- Forgiveness is a conscious decision to let go of what no longer serves us.
- Forgiveness is a gift we give to ourselves.
- Forgiveness sets us free from harmful thoughts, emotions, actions, and others.
- Forgiveness enables us to release the past and live fully in the present.
- Forgiveness is possible.
- Forgiveness is simply a decision we make because we matter.

Forgiveness enables us to better care for ourselves. Harboring anger, hurt, and resentment binds us to those who deeply hurt us. Fear, pride, and martyrdom prevent us from forgiving. Forgiveness is not about condoning another's behavior. It's about not allowing it to overshadow our lives. When we forgive those who have hurt us, we choose to release all that no longer serves us. That allows us to move forward with greater strength, resilience, dignity, and integrity.

The Amish people exhibit a beautiful example of how to live with forgiveness. Years ago, an Amish father and husband, entered a small school in Pennsylvania. He killed multiple children before law enforcement could stop him. It was a horrific incident that impacted so many people. Following that tragedy, the Amish community came together to care for the seriously injured children who did not die, to bury those who died, and to support those who survived. They lovingly and selflessly embraced the murderer's spouse and children and offered them gracious support. The entire community came together as one to care for all who were involved. They cared for each other with love and grace. They forgave the defendant for what he did, and they prioritized healing their community. It remains a very powerful message of forgiveness. How did these devastatingly bereaved individuals find the power to forgive the one who killed and maimed their children and tried to destroy their faith in humanity. I stand in awe of the grace the Amish community displayed and taught us. They focused on loving, healing, and serving others which in turn released the hate, anger, and all that did not serve them. Their actions portray a beautiful example of how to forgive.

When we forgive, we move forward unencumbered with greater peace and freedom. We allow ourselves to heal from the hurt, anger, and resentment that others created. Some people are truly incapable of introspection, and do not feel guilt or remorse. Others are controlling, blaming, shaming, and or disregarding. Still others do not want to change because they think they are perfect and all-knowing. Such people fail to see how their actions hurt others. They often blame others when life is difficult, or not going their way. It's very difficult to understand such people. Yet, it is important to remember their issues are not ours. Knowing that what they do is about them, not us, is vital. We can willing forgive and release them if we want to, and move forward with peace and acceptance in our hearts. We need not be tethered to them anymore.

The more prolonged the pain inflicted, the longer it takes to process the pain caused by others. Painful experiences can easily accumulate and build over time. When harm invades our lives, it causes us to suffer. Through the act of forgiving, we no longer allow unhealthy others to deny our reality, minimize our thoughts and emotions, and negatively impact our lives. We will intuitively know when it's time to move on. Confronting the harmful behaviors of broken people often infuriates them, which leads to more intensive attacks and insults. We must ask ourselves if it is worth our time and energy to address issues with those who are not capable or emotionally mature enough to do so.

Kind people who possess insight, compassion, and remorse can own their hurtful behavior, apologize, and work toward restoring broken relationships. But we are not all the same. Recognizing those who lack insight, are controlling, abusive, and incapable of understanding their negative ways is vital. In their minds, there is no need to look at their own behavior because they are fine. We find people like this in our families, friendships, workplaces, or other circles. As adults, we owe it to ourselves, to avoid or minimize our contact with such people. Children are not as fortunate.

So why forgive? That is the critical question to ask ourselves. We become willing to forgive when we understand that harboring painful experiences binds us to perpetrators. Forgiveness releases us. Forgiving is a conscious decision. When we suffer enough, we often let go of all that no longer serves us. We can decide how much energy we want to expend on difficult issues. Venting is necessary to move on, but we must be careful not to get stuck in it.

Many acts are brutal to forgive, such as murder, rape, abuse, and torture. However, I have learned that whatever the crime, we can choose to let it go. No one deserves to live in pain. If we choose not to let it go, our unwillingness to forgive forever keeps us stuck and bound to the past. It prevents us from living fully and it negatively overshadows our present. Letting go of toxic others creates more space within us to live lives with greater joy and peace.

In my life, I have had many opportunities to practice forgiveness. I married my second husband, who is the father of three beautiful sons. I met my husband's children when they were little boys. Shortly after we got married, problems began and persisted for decades. My role as a stepmother seemed to threaten others. The court ordered custody agreement was 50/50, my husband and

I split the time equally with his children, as did his ex and her husband. The child custody arrangement proved impossible at times despite multiple attempts to have an open, amicable relationship.

I learned early on that being a step-parent can sometimes be a very thankless job. I felt the cliché, "I'm damned if I do and damned if I don't". As conveyed in our family marriage vows, my intentions were to love and respect my husband and stepsons. I, too, wanted the same in return and received it. My husband and stepsons are great. However, endless outside attempts to control our lives created repeated hurt, anger, and anguish.

Controlling, insecure people are not emotionally or mentally healthy. Their fierce determination and need to control others is how they escape their own issues and painful pasts. The nature of those who need to control others is an addiction that helps them to avoid their painful pasts. The more controlling the person, the greater the pain and shame they carry. Insecure people put others down in order to feel better about themselves or bond with others in unhealthy ways. Insecure people are dangerous and contribute to creating great pain and toxicity in the world. Happy people have no need to control or put down others because they possess self-worth.

I learned and must remember that living in anger, resentment, and unforgiveness robs me of happiness. I strive to release emotions, thoughts, and attitudes that do not serve me or enhance my life. I ask for God's help to become willing to forgive and release those who have hurt me. It is a struggle at times but the alternative results in being lost in an abyss of negativity. I chose to live in a more positive world. A friend of mine said, "It's easy to be miserable. It's more difficult to be happy." Refusing to forgive is draining, exhausting, and stressful. I also pray for the health, peace, love, and joy for those who love me and also for those who hurt me. If they find happiness, the world is a better place. I also utilize prayers of protection against darkness and evil.

The struggle to forgive is challenging. It is difficult to forgive those who cause us and those we love pain. But, it's a decision to love ourselves. Living in anger and resentment prevents us from living. We must work diligently to release negative thoughts and emotions.

Hurtful people will continue to impact our lives, but we control our reactions. Hurtful others are not worth my happiness. I will continue to pray they heal and find happiness. I choose not to keep company with them. Nor do I wish them harm. I accept that I'm not sure I can ever understand why such people do what they do or why they do not seek help. Yet, it doesn't matter. I can only protect myself and focus on living the life I truly love.

Learning to forgive ourselves is also important. We suffer from the mistakes we make. We are human. But mistakes can help us to understand ourselves better and to grow. Learning to forgive ourselves is a necessary act of kindness we all deserve.

My cancer diagnosis propels me to release all that doesn't serve me. If my time on earth is limited, I refuse to waste my time on what I cannot change. All that does is steal my joy and happiness. It is genuinely not worth it. Cancer forces me to ask myself on a daily basis what it is I would like to do should today be my last one on earth. We do not need life-threatening diagnoses to think like this. Any of us can die today. So, what are we waiting for?

What we think about is what we bring about. What we resist persists. These sayings have been around for years. We can focus our thoughts on all that empowers us and feeds our soul. We can surround ourselves with those who love and support us well. We can forgive because it sets us free. We must cease hurting ourselves. We must learn to love ourselves and others well. If we are sincere in our attempts to create the best lives we can, we must forgive ourselves and others and move forward with love and peace in our hearts.

It is important to not take the words and actions of others personally or to make assumptions about their behavior. Actions are always about the person performing them. Life is too short. Let's choose our battles carefully, for some are just not worth our time and energy. Asking our Higher Power to release us from all that does not serve us. Learn to be compassionate with ourselves. Forgiveness enables us to create space to become ALL WE ARE BORN TO BE.

CHAPTER 6

SPIRITUALITY

"Happiness cannot be traveled to, owned, earned, worn, or consumed. Happiness is the spiritual experience of living every minute with love, grace, and gratitude."
– Denis Waitley

It is within the silence of being still and quiet that we come to know who and what we are. When we quiet our minds and thoughts to hear our inner guidance, we will hear the whispers of God. A consistent, daily spiritual practice helps us to create a conscious, purposeful, and meaningful lives. A spiritual practice can be as little as fifteen minutes a day, preferably in the morning, because it sets the tone for the day. Prayer, meditation, and gratitude enhances our lives. Consistency is important. The more we do it, the better we become at discerning the voice of God within from our own thoughts.

Growing up in an unpredictable and chaotic home, I grew to appreciate the quiet times when I could hear my own thoughts and shut out outside influences. Silence enhances our ability to be fully present in the moment. In silence, we create safe, grounded moments. My dear friend Michele says that the trees, flowers, and grasses grow in silence and find the light. It's true for us as well. When we quiet ourselves, the wisdom within can guide us.

Silence, or quiet meditation, helps us to release our thoughts and hear the wisdom of God within. The spiritual wisdom that guides us to our passions and purposes. Without heeding our inner guidance, our overactive brain often floats from one thing to the next. We quickly get lost in the shuffle of life without ever realizing it. When we quiet our minds, we allow space for divine guidance to arise. At the beginning of our spiritual practice, we may question what we hear, but in time, we become adept at discerning our voice from the wisdom within.

When I was a second grader in Catholic School, I remember my teacher, a Catholic nun, teaching our class about God. I remember her sharing that God is watching us and frowns when we are imperfect. I quietly disagreed. I had already developed a good relationship with God, who I knew didn't judge, persecute, or punish us. I believed in God's love, forgiveness, and grace. I trusted God because people frightened and disappointed me. I believed God wants us to be happy, loved, and have free will. God can and will help us to think and act better.

Sadly, many religions teach about a punitive, punishing, or revengeful God. God is none of these things. People often spew their personal interpretations of God or the bible. Developing a private spiritual practice helps us to transcend all that. Without faith in something greater than ourselves, we often feel lost and alone. I wonder how people make sense of their world when they do not believe in something greater than themselves.

Establishing a spiritual practice enhances all aspects of our lives. We can learn from experiences because they often have much to teach us. We must become willing and open to learn. We can ask God what we are to learn from any experience. No two spiritual paths are alike. What works for me may not work for you, and vice versa. Establish a practice that works for you and fuels your soul.

My spiritual practice begins with one or more daily devotions. I read and think about how the devotions relate to my life. Devotional books input positive messages into my life. Following the readings, I read a few prayers from Marianne Williamson's Illuminata book, whichever ones speak to me that day. I also have a list of people I pray for daily. I then sit in silent meditation and listen for divine guidance on how I can better serve and do my part each day. Lastly, I write at least three or more things for which I am grateful. Gratitude and thankfulness change our attitude and enable us to focus on the good things in our lives. We cannot be grateful and negative at the same time. Choose gratitude.

Prayer and meditation link us to the power and wisdom within that assists us to creating lives with greater intention, purpose, meaning, and empowerment. The incessant chatter within our minds often takes us off track. In silence, we find our way. Prayer is our talking to God. Meditation is God's response to us. Gratitude promotes a positive, daily mindset and helps us to focus on what is truly important in our lives, such as health, peace, love, shelter, food, and more.

A spiritual practice enhances our relationship with ourselves, others, and our higher power. The relationship with our higher power is like any other relationship. What we put into it is what we get out of it. Voicing our wants, desires, and struggles is essential. How does God know what we need or desire if we don't ask? The greater the clarity of what we desire, the greater the possibility for it to manifest. Knowing ourselves and what we desire requires effort and thought. It is our responsibility. Totally understanding ourselves and what we love and need is essential to the creation of living meaningful and purposeful lives. We are uniquely different from each other and have specific gifts to offer others. We are equal in the eyes of God.

Marianne Williamson writes, "Sacred energy renews us." Cultivating a spiritual practice enables us to find peace, and to grow and become all we are born to be. Without it, life is mere existence. Taking responsibility for knowing ourselves and what we desire requires a lot of inner work. We need to take the time to sort out what is important to us, what we want to do with our lives, and how we can manifest the same. It's work that many of us will shun because it challenges us to think deeply about our lives, relationships, and where we are. If we find ourselves feeling complacent or unhappy, we possess the power to change it. Change requires work and commitment. It is easier to go with the flow and perhaps do what others desire us to do or to be who others want us to be. The ultimate question is, are we being true to ourselves? If we desire peace, purpose, and meaning in our lives, we must do our part and help ourselves. We can act our way into better thinking and living. Spiritual guidance transforms our lives in every way.

One's spirituality is very personal. It's essential to create and cultivate a personal spiritual practice that works for us. Once we develop a practice, take notice of how our lives change for the better. God is with us and wants to help us to become all we are born to be. Remember, we are a small part of the universal whole. Prayer and meditation are powerful tools to utilize to assist us along the way. Are you living a life that you love? Are you sharing your gifts to help yourself and others grow? Let's strive to become all we are meant to be.

In addition to prayer, I practice gratitude. We live in a world of people who see the glass half empty instead of half full. Gratitude fills that glass with positivity. It is so important to pay close attention to what we focus on daily. So many people are glued to news stations, games, Facebook, Instagram, emails, texts, and more. The time we spend on our phones or the internet often takes us further and further away from ourselves. There is a great deal of negativity in our world. It's important to be conscious of what we expose ourselves to.

Gratitude counters negativity. An easy way to practice gratitude is to keep a journal and each day, identify three or more things we are grateful for. In the beginning, it may be challenging but the more we practice it, the easier it gets. Ideas to be grateful for is the ability to breathe, walk, work, play, raise children, study, friends, opportunities, and so on. The more we do it, the greater our positivity and gratitude we build. We cannot be grateful and miserable or negative at the same time. Gratitude and thankfulness for all we have is how we begin to create the lives we love.

Listening to the whisperings within leads us to greater joy, meaning and purpose. Without a spiritual practice, we can easily get caught up in meaningless tasks every day. Our purpose is needed to help others along their way. Each and every one of us have so much to offer each other. It doesn't matter what we believe in as much as it does to believe in something greater than ourselves. Spirituality uplifts us and offers us hope for a better tomorrow.

CHAPTER 7

THE
SCARS WITHIN

"The body keeps the score."
– Bessel van der Kolk

Unprocessed wounds and emotions are embedded in our minds, the cells in our bodies, and our souls. Present-day life challenges can trigger buried hurts and emotions, which cause them to bubble up and burst into our present. When that occurs, we often overreact to present circumstances rather than simply respond. During such times, being with ourselves can feel overwhelming. The intensity of our emotions can be frightening. Many of us will repress, deny, or escape our feelings because we fear they are too much to handle. The build-up of emotions escalates our fears. We must remember that our feelings will not make us crazy or harm us. I promise. We may think our feelings will cause us to go off the deep end, but they won't. Instead, if we embrace our feelings and allow them to surface, they will dissipate quicker. Resisting, repressing, or denying our emotions will increase their intensity and make them more challenging to deal with later on. Our unresolved issues and repressed emotions will wreak havoc in our present lives and relationships. Often, we project our unconscious issues onto those we love.

A mountain of built-up emotions overwhelms us. Eventually, our pent-up feelings will burst out. The more we deny our emotions, the greater the eruption. The more explosive we react, the more frightened we feel. It takes tremendous courage to face our issues and process our emotions. We can learn to release our feelings in healthy and productive ways.

Years ago, I taught elementary-age school children with special needs. I had a class of six children between the ages of five and eleven years old, all classified as emotionally disturbed.

One day, a six-year-old little child who was struggling and began to suddenly act out in class. Attempts to calm him were unsuccessful. He was angry, and his behavior quickly escalated and was volatile. He started to throw things and destroy things in our classroom. He ripped-up papers, pushed everything off desks, and began to throw or destroy anything he could get he could find. His reasoning ability was gone. He threatened our safety. Keeping the class safe was my priority. I ushered the other five students out of the classroom door to safety. Through the window in the door, I watched him further explode. He knocked over desks, threw chairs, and violently lashed out. He lifted my big, old, heavy metal teacher's desk off the floor. Attempts to defuse him were unsuccessful. He was raging and was dangerous to himself and others. He lost control. In time, he began to tire and slow down. He began to hear us trying to help him. Once exhausted, he became more reasonable.

This little guy released a mountain of unresolved pain and anger which burst into his presence for no detectible reason. Afterwards, he was referred to counseling to help him better manage his emotions and behavior. He had no history of volatile behavior, but something triggered his emotional release. The classroom was calm and stable before the incident began.

This story exemplifies how unresolved emotions can erupt when we have not yet learned healthy coping skills. This young child had not yet developed an understanding of his emotions. His coping skills were minimal at the time. Due to his age, he was unable to understand abstract concepts such as emotions. He did not yet have adequate coping skills to manage his feelings. So many wounded children are unfairly labeled as emotionally disturbed because of their inability to deal with their pain.

When I was thirty-one years old, I entered a treatment center for alcoholics and addicts and also for those with a history of trauma. During that time, I participated in a week-long workshop to help survivors deal with past emotional, physical, and sexual abuse. In the 1980s, understanding childhood trauma and PTSD, Post Traumatic Stress Disorder, was just beginning to be understood and explored. PTSD was widely understood and accepted when dealing with war-torn soldiers, but at that time it was not often associated with childhood trauma.

Shortly after entering the seven-day treatment workshop addressing the impact of emotional, physical, and sexual abuse, many of my childhood memories of abuse surfaced. There were moments, I struggled to breathe due to intense pain and anxiety, despite having two supportive therapists at my side. A flood of buried thoughts, images, and emotions from my past enveloped me. It was beyond overwhelming. I wasn't sure I could get through it. I entertained thoughts of death, but I was too scared to act on them. The intensity of my upcoming emotions terrified me. As I allowed my feelings to surface and be released, I was able to better manage my thoughts and behavior. Eventually, the emotions lessened, as did my fears of living.

Repressed trauma is like a shook-up can of soda ready to explode at any time. I experienced that explosion of memories, emotions, and more. For me, it was decades of repressed pain and anguish. Unlike my former young student, I was more equipped to deal with the mountain of emotion. It wasn't easy. I needed tremendous support. It was intense, but I had an advantage. I had a better understanding of my emotions and possessed greater coping skills than those of my former student.

Our bodies automatically store the experiences and emotions we fail to process along the way. If not dealt with appropriately, we may unfairly blame or scapegoat others in our present life for the anguish we feel, despite it being an old wound. We can only run so far. The longer we postpone processing our issues, the more complicated and dysfunctional our lives become. Buried wounds often negatively taint all aspects of our lives.

I've learned a lot from my past experiences. I wish I knew then what I do now. I escaped life for a long, long time. I learned that failing to deal with my issues when they occur, they will surely build and inappropriately impact my present life. Seeking support at such times is essential and helpful. I learned that choosing to do it alone makes my life more difficult and often unmanageable. I learned that my emotions will not kill me, regardless of intensity. I learned that when I deal with my issues, I make more room for joy and positivity in my life. I learned that the worst was over, and I could deal with my experiences without falling apart. I learned that counseling, physical activity, prayer, meditation, and bodywork are great tools to help me process traumatic experiences more efficiently and healthily.

Processing buried wounds and emotions takes time, energy, courage, and commitment. Personal and professional support helps tremendously. Body/energy therapies, such as massage, reiki, yoga, cranial sacral, and acupuncture, help us heal in healthy ways. Counseling support offers us a better perspective and fuels hope. Exercise takes the edge off the intensity of our emotions. Did you ever go for a walk or run when you were angry? By the time we finish, we are often less reactive than before we started. Nutrition and diet significantly impact how we feel, sleep, and perform. Our mind, body, and soul are interconnected, and we cannot heal one without regard for the others. We may manage symptoms, but healing requires more.

All inner wounds do not present as explosively as the above experiences. But, if we fail to process our emotions and experiences as they occur, they are guaranteed to build and eventually erupt. Our unresolved issues often hurt the ones we love. Our words can quickly become weapons. Although our minds may not remember, our bodies store our history. Our bodies house every bit of our history, the good and the bad.

There's a lot written about the effects of combat on mental health. Childhood trauma has a very similar impact. Often, the very people children rely can hurt and sometimes kill them. There's no way out because children's lives depend on their caregivers. Their bodies are small, and everything and everyone is bigger, stronger, more powerful, etc. Childhood trauma is often chronic, not one but many incidents. Children may not have the tools or support to help them process their emotions and experiences. Children are vulnerable and often powerless. Trauma embeds into their little beings as they strive to survive and make sense of their chaotic, often dangerous world.

Young children are developmentally incapable of dealing with complex emotions. They depend on adults for love, care, and protection. In abusive homes, primary needs are often unmet, let alone emotional needs. Children act out their emotions in trying to deal with them. Acting out behaviors often increases their chances of further abuse. Childhood trauma is pervasive and deadly.

It's essential to also highlight lesser assaults against children. Those of us who may have grown up in functional yet emotionally limited or neglectful families struggle too. It is sometimes more challenging for these survivors to admit the harm inflicted. Some people tend to minimize and excuse their difficult experiences because comparatively, other situations seem far worse than their own. Neglect, scapegoating, sexual exploitation, incompetent parenting, and significantly destroy children's lives. As a former therapist, I've worked with wounded adults who minimize or deny their painful histories and the impact it has on their present lives. In doing so, they psychologically and developmentally get stuck and fail to grow.

Acknowledging our past and how it impacts the present is essential for healing and growth. Blaming others keeps us stuck. Trying to understand those who hurt us may give us a false sense of safety, but it does not help us grow or live healthy lives. Instead, it impedes growth and disables us from becoming more.

We are who we are because of our caregivers and are impacted by who they were who they weren't. We, too, have the potential to hurt others in ways we have experienced. We learned how words become weapons and cause great pain. Yet, we have the potential to become more. We can choose to learn better ways to deal with life and stress. We need not act-out our histories inappropriately and perpetuate abuse.

If we examine our lives and relationships, most would agree that we could do better. We may not know how to help ourselves. That is why therapy is so important. Meeting with someone who can be objective provides us another perspective to see and evaluate ourselves and others. Seeking counseling does not mean we are crazy. Counseling helps us to treat ourselves and others in healthier ways. It means that what we are taking responsibility for our ourselves and our behavior. If what we are doing is not working, then how do we expect things are going to change? The stigma of pursuing therapy prevents us from learning and growing. No one has all the answers. In therapy, we often find the answers for ourselves.

Everyone is unique and heals in their way. There is not a one-size-fits-all solution. As a former therapist, I strived to help others by redirecting them back to themselves and their inner guidance. I offered life tools to help. The answers are within us. Leading people back to themselves is critical. Helping others connect with their inner wisdom, as opposed to someone else's. We have all we will ever need within to grow, blossom, and become all we are born to be.

Many of us need outside support to understand and learn better ways to cope. That is why I encourage people to go to therapy. Personal growth requires courage, commitment, and dedication. We must find the courage to create better and healthier lives. We must be willing to shake, rattle and roll if necessary. We must cease blaming, learn to forgive, and release the past.

We can heal from anything if we chose to do so. The wounds and scars can make or break us. It's our choice. There's no excuse to stay where we are or to give up. There are many healthy ways to grow and become all we are born to be. When we choose not to heal, we fail ourselves. We deserve a worthy, happy, meaningful life. We have everything we will ever need to heal our wounds, live fully, share our gifts, and find the courage to create lives we love.

CHAPTER 8

THE
FACES OF
ANGER

*"To be angry is to revenge the faults of
others on ourselves."*
– By Alexander Pope

Anger is a normal feeling, but sometimes it can be a dangerous emotion if we allow it to build within us. Beneath our anger is pain, often deep pain. The actions of others will sometimes hurt us. The positive attribute of anger is that it is energizing. When angry, we often get a lot done. When sad, we withdraw, isolate, and feel lethargic. Anger fuels us in many ways, whereas sadness drains us.

I have older twin brothers, David, and Jeff. David was charismatic, capable, friendly, funny, intelligent, handsome, and likable. These words describe David when he was sober. David was also an active alcoholic for much of his adult life. David was thirty-five years old when his health issues began. His inability to stay sober prevented him from living fully and creating a successful, meaningful life.

At age 35, he married and was very happy. At his wedding, he was the picture of health, dressed in all white. He was fit, tan, attractive, and looked so vibrant and healthy. All night, the blue-eyed, blond, sober groom danced the night away. He and his wife dreamed of happily ever after.

A few months after his wedding, David sought medical attention because of serious pain in his leg. A series of tests, scans, and examinations determined his cardiovascular system was not functioning well to supply blood to needed parts of his body. We are unsure if a serious tractor incident he was injured in when he was a teen caused the problem. Perhaps it was chronic alcoholism, or a bit of both. Regardless, that was the beginning of his horrendous, ten-year health battle resulting in devastating, life-altering surgeries, and numerous hospitalizations.

David's legs were amputated piece by piece until he was left with small stumps where his legs had been. His prostheses grew bigger and heavier, making it even more challenging to walk. Eventually, he became wheelchair-dependent. After the loss of his legs, David escaped more and more into alcoholism to avoid his pain, anger, and anguish. He was brutally heartbroken when intoxicated and inconsolable. Yet when sober, he was vibrant and optimistic. Alcoholism is a severe disease that impacts all who love the alcoholic.

From age 40 to 45 years old, David was relatively stable. But he was never the same after he lost his legs. Shortly after his 45th birthday, he was once again hospitalized for stomach issues, or so we thought. The doctors determined that his vascular problems progressed to the trunk of his body. The blood supply to his is intestines were no longer supplying the volume of blood need to his body. More surgeries followed because his body lacked the needed oxygen to heal. David was bandaged from his throat to his groin—multiple tubes protruded from his body.

He remained in ICU from October to December. He had no advanced directives. My mom struggled not to lose her third child, and his son wanted everything done to save his dad. The doctors medically paralyzed David because his body's drug tolerance was so high, they feared increased pain medication would hasten his death.

David died on December 11, 1992. I felt so angry and heartbroken. I believed David could have been anything he wanted to be if he tried harder. I was clean and sober, so why couldn't he do the same? He was loved by so many people. The loss of his legs took a horrendous mental, emotional, physical, and spiritual toll on him. He tried so many times to maintain sobriety, but couldn't. When drunk, he would verbally mourn the loss of his legs. It was utterly devastating to witness. He was capable, even without legs. He drove, repaired car engines, patched my mom's leaking roof, and generally exhibited an outwardly optimistic outlook. On the inside, alcohol helped him to repress and bury a mountain of pain, anger, and deep grief. His wife left him shortly after his health problems began, months after their marriage. She could not tolerate his drinking.

The summer before David died, he came to visit me in Tennessee. Of course, he got drunk on the plane but he did stay sober throughout the rest of his stay. He befriended my neighbors and often cooked for them. Because I worked over 60 hours a week, I barely saw, let alone knew my neighbors. But my brother was a people magnet. He was very friendly. People loved him. Before long, he befriended several of my neighbors.

David loved to fish, so we planned a fishing trip during his visit. To my apartment front door, I had many steps leading down from the parking lot to a flat, cement landing and then there were more steps up to my front door. When coming or going, David would wheel himself down the steps and around the corner of the parking lot to an adjacent side street. The path was flatter for him to wheel himself to the side street. He found it was easier to manage in his wheelchair taking that route. Once on the street, David wheeled to or from my apartment. An incident that stayed has stayed with me for years happened one morning when as I was leaving my apartment. I locked my apartment door and turned around to see David sitting on the dirt by steps leading up to the parking area. When I asked him what he was doing, he responded that he was looking for something on the ground. Then, quickly he hopped back into his wheelchair as if nothing happened. As he hopped up into his wheel chair, I noticed dirt on his entire right side and realized he must have tried to take a shorter route to the car and fallen out of his wheelchair. I suspect he was too embarrassed or ashamed to tell me he fell. It was a heartbreaking and eye-opening moment. David never talked about the challenges of being wheelchair bound. He hid his emotions when sober and did not talk about how difficult his life was without his legs. He struggled to accept emotional and physical support, even from his loved ones. He protected those he loved from his heartache.

On October 1st of that same year, I drove to New Jersey to bury my father. I knew David was in the hospital but I was told it was his stomach issues. He remained in ICU for the next eight weeks and rapidly declined. David died just four months after his Tennessee vacation.

I was so angry and heartbroken about my brother's death for a long time. I was mad at his alcoholism and the tremendous pain it caused our family. My brother was brilliant and touched many people in his life and death. Why couldn't he stay sober? Through his chaotic sobriety struggle, I came to a greater understanding of alcoholism as a disease. Some of us will live, yet many of us will die. For years, I had hoped and prayed for my brother's sobriety. I was emotionally and mentally exhausted from wanting more for David than he did for himself.

It's been near three decades since David's death. I sometimes still feel residual emotions of paining sorrow. I've shed mountains of tears and felt my heart break open after his death. The impact of his life and death lingers. I miss him.

Anger has many faces. For far too many years of my life, I exhibited a tough exterior. It was how I learned to protect myself from pain and anguish. It's a habit I learned to slowly release, for I now know better ways. I no longer need to distance myself from others or the pain within. I know I am safe. I know I am not alone. Many people exhibit tough exteriors. Yet, beneath their defensiveness is great pain.

Beneath our anger lies tremendous pain. Because anger is energizing, we tend to hang onto it. Pain is debilitating and often requires more from us. We get a lot done when we are angry. Pain and anguish deplete our energy, robs our sleep, and frequently impedes our sense of hope. For men, anger is the more accepted emotion. Angry females are often labeled bitches. Likewise, men are often viewed as wimpy when they express their pain and sadness. For some of us, anger may be an easier emotion to deal with because of its energizing impact. Pain and sorrow do the opposite, drain us. So many other emotions lie hidden beneath our anger.

It takes great courage and strength to process our angry and pain. Yet, what we resist will continue to persist in our lives. Our identity is forever tainted by that which we avoid. Feeling and processing our emotions and experiences are difficult, but doable. To heal, we must allow ourselves to feel. The more we accept our feelings, the quicker we heal.

Years ago, I labeled those who cried easily as wimpy. Today, I've learned to respect those so-called wimpy individuals because of the tremendous courage it requires to be open and vulnerable. and willing to reach out for support. It took years of suffering before I learned how to own my emotions and allow myself to lean on others. My husband has repeatedly expressed his concerns about my inability to ask for help. Asking for help often doesn't occur naturally for me because I have cracks in my foundation. I had to learn to express my emotions in healthy ways and to understand that it is normal to seek help. Despite decades of living with a supportive spouse, I sometimes still struggle with dealing with my experiences alone. It's a well-developed survival skill that has served me for many years. I now know better and must work to release the need to be alone, because it does not help or serve me.

Anger frightens people when it is reactive and abusive. We can and must learn ways to express it without harming ourselves or others. We have a right to voice our anger. We have a right to be heard when we feel hurt and angry. Yet we must not attack or blame others when we are hurt, anger, or betrayed. Instead, we can learn to maturely express our thoughts and emotions without persecuting others. It is important to let others know how their actions hurt us. Not everyone will honor our emotions, and that is okay. That is their issue. That is why it is so important to truly evaluate who we give our hearts to hold.

I was quick to anger over the years and knew well how to hurt others with words. But doing that only hurt and shamed me and caused more suffering. I knew how to hide my vulnerability from others. But I work diligently to learn healthier ways to process and express my anger without hurting myself or others. I realized hurting others hurt me, too. I know words can be powerful weapons and I must be careful when expressing anger or pain. Seeking support and help from others gives me tools to better manage my life and cease creating unnecessary suffering for myself or others.

Prayer also enables me to express my emotions with less blame and self-righteousness. Prayer enables me to help myself. Sometimes my anger has been directed at God. I refused to pray and wanted nothing to do with God. However, the more I blamed God or others, the more I suffered. Exploring the pain beneath my anger enables me to release it in less hurtful ways. Utilizing therapy to find healthier ways to express my words and feelings helped me progress and move toward better living. I learned better ways to be in my world.

David's death triggered so much anger in me toward his alcoholism and inability to stay sober. I blamed him for dying. I blamed him for making stupid decisions that hastened his death. I've come to a better understand alcoholism as a real disease today. I've learned much from my anger. I learned how my anger prevented me from processing my own pain and anguish. I loved my brother deeply. I miss him. I no longer want to carry heavy, unprocessed emotions. I want to feel and release my emotions and be set free. Unprocessed issues keep us living in the past. It's our responsibility to feel and heal. Healing awaits us all if we dare to embrace our emotions.

Another technique I learned over the years to release anger and let it go is by acting. I could write a raging letter to the person telling them everything they did that caused me pain. I could then read it to a therapist or friend for validation, and then destroy it. The offending person never sees it. What I find buried beneath the anger is usually a lot of hurt. Crying released the intensity of my anger. Prayer helped me to defuse my anger and embrace my pain. There are many other ways to release anger and pain in healthy ways. We must learn to find ways that work for us. We may not have the opportunity to work through it with those who caused it, and that's okay. Anger deeply binds us to our past and prevents us from creating the lives we love. Anger and pain are not worth carrying around. It is too disruptive and detrimental to our well-being. We let go of all that prevents us from becoming all we are born to be. We deserve to live meaningful and healthy lives.

CHAPTER 9

ADDICTIONS

"I came. I came to. I came to believe"
– Anonymous

Addictions impact all of us. Active addictions prevent us from growing emotionally, mentally, and spiritually. Addictions enable us to escape life and repress what we want to avoid. Addictions disconnect us from ourselves, others, and God. Addictions include drugs, alcohol, shopping, overworking, excessive exercising, overeating, anorexia, screen time on our phones, commuters and television, gambling, smoking, vaping, and more. Many addictions are legal and often go unnoticed, but the result is the same. Addictions prevent us from feeling and dealing with life issues. We fail to grow unless we escape into whatever we overdo. Rather than creating lives we love, we remain stuck in our self-created mess. Blaming others is an excuse to shun taking responsibility for ourselves and the lives we desire to create. Addictions enable us to repress our emotions, hide behind our issues, escape our relationships, and so m much more.

Life is great, but at times. it is very challenging. 12-Step programs often profess that what we resist will persist. When we resist feeling our emotions, they build within us. Sooner or later, we face a mountain of repressed emotions or issues that often feels overwhelming and frightening. We may think we cannot handle our feelings or we are unable to control them. But the reality is our emotions will not kill us or cause insanity. Our emotions can take our breath away, make our hearts beat faster, depress us, immobilize us, cause insomnia, cause us to react in inappropriate ways and create health issues. Yet, we will not die from feeling our emotions. The intensity of our emotions lessens as we accept and embrace them and allow them to flow and go.

All health issues have an emotional origin. In Louise Hay's book, You Can Heal Your Life, she identifies the emotional causes of physical problems. She also shares beautiful life-affirming affirmations to counter negative thoughts. Hay says all of us struggle with guilt, shame, unworthiness, and criticism to some extent and we must come to terms with those issues. Our bodies serve as a great barometer to let us know when we are not okay. We experience aches, pain, insomnia, fatigue, etc., when we avoid unresolved issues. Listening to our bodies is necessary to better care for ourselves and live healthier lives.

On June 6th, 1988, at 31 years old, I stopped drinking alcohol. I ceased using drugs nine years prior. Within a few days of being sober, I was admitted to a dual substance abuse program that addressed addictions and trauma. While I was in treatment, a ton of emotions and trauma came bursting out. I felt as if I was going to die. I wanted to die. Memories of mental, physical, and emotional trauma surface. It was one of the darkest times of my life. The treatment therapists promised me that if I would cease fighting the intense release of emotions and memories, it would get better. Gradually, I found the courage to feel my terrifying, intense emotions. Sobriety was very challenging but I knew deep inside that I needed to heal if wanted a happier and healthier life.

I began drinking alcohol at 11 years old. I didn't like the taste of alcohol, but I loved how it allowed me to escape. It wasn't much later that I found drugs which offered me a similar escape. In addition to alcohol and drugs, I discovered that codependency, overworking, and food also aided me in escaping life. I drank and got high to stifle the pain within me. If I drank, I got drunk. If I did drugs, it was until I fell asleep or became unconscious. I was ill-equipped to deal with my life completely sober. My thoughts and emotions were too much for me to handle. I needed a ton of support to even stay in my own skin. I attended thousand of 12-Step meetings, did therapy, energy work, and anything I could think of to live.

I entertained the idea of death often. Although I wasn't actively suicidal, I used substances like I was. Drugs and alcohol were needed to escape my reality of my life. Alcoholism was in my family history. The people in recovery truly loved me until I could learn to love myself. Without them, I doubt I would be here. They were my lifeline.

The 12-Step program is a spiritual program. It is not affiliated with any religion or creed, but alludes to a power greater than ourselves. One is free to define their own higher power, be it a God, nature, or whatever. I had nothing to lose by asking a power greater than myself to help me. I was at a dead end without options. The 12-Steps helped me to manage my mountain of emotions. In recovery rooms, people shrugged off my craziness and told me to keep coming back and promised me things would get better. I came back because I had nowhere else to go and didn't know what to do. In time, my loneliness and craziness began to lessen. Those selfless recovering alcoholics and addicts saved my life.

They truly loved me until I learned to love myself. The people in the 12-Step programs are incredibly resilient, forgiving, compassionate, caring, loving people. Most importantly, they believed in me. They believed in what I could become. I am beyond blessed to have found such accepting, beautiful people who lived tremendously difficult lives and were from all walks of life -- rich, poor, wealthy, broke, black, white, yellow, etc. These people accepted and welcomed me in all my brokenness. Sitting in the rooms of people who are recovering keeps me ever humble, grateful, and grounded.

I learned so much during that time in my life. I learned there are many ways to escape life beyond drugs and alcohol. I learned I am very sensitive and life easily hurts me. I learned seeking solace in using substances delayed my healing and could have killed me. I learned intense emotions are manageable with professional support and human kindness. I learned how to have fun and enjoy life sober. I realized I am the same person inside that I always was, and it's okay to be me. I learned that my emotions are not to be feared regardless of how intense they feel. I learned to connect deeply with a power beyond myself that guides me toward better living. I learned to let go and allow God to lead the way because my life was often unmanageable.

Addictions enable us to escape ourselves and our issues. We judge one another, but the truth is that we are alike in many ways. Not all will go to the depths of despair, but many of us are guilty of running from ourselves. Until we summon the courage to face ourselves and process our emotions, we fail to grow and to be true to ourselves. Very few, if any, of us will escape childhood without some wounds. Our wounds are our spiritual lessons. Some of us endured brutal trauma and likely need additional support to heal. Until we learn to lean on loving and accepting others until we feel alone and fragile. Life can be difficult which means we will all struggle at times.

The real question is, do we want to be victims or survivors? The choice is ours. The power and strength we need is always within us. We are as alone as we choose to be. Regardless of our difficult experiences or the harm we caused ourselves or others, we can and must believe that healing is possible. Healing is a decision. Healing requires commitment. We can heal and create healthier lives. Negative experiences cause us to be stronger and resilient, more than we ever imagined. The past is over and can't hurt us anymore. We need not allow it to suck the life out of us and rob us of joy. That was then, and this is now. Now is the time to assume full responsibility to heal the cracks in our foundations and release what no longer serves us. Trust and know deeply that we can heal and become all we are born to be. We owe it to ourselves and each other to live authentically and courageously. We no longer need to escape. We have the power to change our lives whenever we so decide. It's up to us.

CHAPTER 10

THE CRACKS IN OUR
FOUNDATIONS

"It's easy to look at people and make quick judgments about their present and past, but you'd be amazed at the pain and tears a single smile hides. What a person shows is only one tiny facet of an iceberg hidden from sight. And more often than not, it's lined with cracks and scars that go all the way to the soul."
– Sherrilyn Kenyon

In an ideal environment, parents and caregivers help children to grow and flourish by creating a solid foundation of love, support, and consistency. As children develop, they learn to trust and depend on others in healthy and productive ways. Children learn about themselves and the world from those who care for them. Yet, many parents do not know how to adequately provide for their children's needs and wants. Many parents and caregivers are wounded from their own experiences, which in turn gets passed on to their children in a repetitive cycle of hurting others. Parents cannot give their children what they themselves have never had or been given unless they healed.

The dysfunctional life cycle of people hurting people continues until we take responsibility for healing ourselves and the world around us. We must learn to embrace ourselves with love, acceptance, compassion, and kindness. Doing so requires us to take responsibility for all of who we are, the good and the not-so-good. Blaming others is a cop-out to not deal with our issues. There is no excuse to harm others or ourselves.

It has taken me decades to understand myself and how I am in the world. I continue to learn about myself and my relationships. At times I still struggle with negative thoughts about myself and the world. Self-love, acceptance, and forgiveness of self and others takes time, effort, and commitment to change and let go of what no longer serves us. We must strive to find healthier and more humane ways to be in our world.

My parents did the best they could with what they knew at the time I was growing up. Yet it was not good enough at times. Their words and actions were violent when they were drunk. They were often overwhelmed and ill-equipped to deal with life. Their wounds significantly impacted them. They struggled in their relationship and escaped through alcohol and other addictions. Their behavior and child rearing are a reflection of their histories. They did not seem to have received the appropriate love and care children need. I don't blame my parents for their issues, but their history left them unprepared to deal with life in healthy ways. Adults make decisions that impact their ability to cope with stress. My parents the seemingly lack of consistent, loving, nurturing milieus, there were gaps or cracks in their foundations. They, like many of us, struggled to cope with life when stressors accumulate. Subsequently, many of us plow through life without examining ourselves and our relationships. We fail to learn how to deal with stress in heathy ways. We mistreat others as we do ourselves until we learn better

Cracks in our foundation occur when children do not consistently feel safe, loved, and nurtured. Fundamental needs often go unmet. Cracks develop when a person's unresolved issues accumulate and often negatively harm theirselves and others. The greater the harm, the deeper the cracks.

Children rely on the adults in their life to survive. If primary and emotional needs for food, shelter, love, safety, and nurturing go unmet, children naturally develop ways to protect themselves to survive. Emotional and physical needs are necessary for healthy growth and development. Research proves that babies whose physical needs are met but lack love and nurturing will often develop a failure to thrive syndrome and die. Abused and neglected babies/children die as well.

Trauma, abuse, and neglect occurs in the lives of children more than we want to see or admit. Some children experience unbelievable physical, emotional, mental, and sexual assaults. They may survive, but the toll of abuse and neglect often leaves them with deep wounds and scars. All experiences are embedded in our physical and emotional bodies until we feel safe enough for the emotions to surface. Many abused children become addicts, prostitutes, or abusers in an attempt to deal with life and survival.

Sometimes I still struggle with the cracks in my foundation. Although I have been safe for decades, my old wounds can sometimes impact my present life and relationships. Although my cracks are not as deep as they once were, they can negatively impact my life when they surface. When caught in a crack, I am in fight mode and take everything personally. I react instead of responding to present situations. I often retreat into myself. I learned that it takes time for me to feel safe. I often want to flee conflict and go somewhere to be with myself. Early into my relationship with my husband, a simple argument could sometimes trigger a highly reactive response from me. I've given him my heart. My unresolved inner unhealed wounds can be triggered when I feel hurt by his words, actions, or lack thereof. Sometimes, the pain of my past will suddenly flood into a present situation, and I may be more reactive than the situation warrants.

In those moments, I forget he loves me. I feel alone and isolated. Words of comfort or sorrow bypass me because the pain within me overshadows the present situation. It is sometimes difficult to sort out the past from my present. I struggle to remember he is not the enemy nor the cause of all my pain and anguish. Conflicts often trigger unresolved issues for us to be healed and released. Relationships can easily ignite our inner fears and wounds because unconsciously we will gravitate toward those who can help us heal our past.

What I have learned about myself in such situations is that it is understandable why I react instead of respond. I must remember that my past is over, and I can protect myself as an adult. I need not allow my wounded inner child to take over and sabotage my life. The internal acting-out child within often inappropriately acts out. When I sense that a present situation triggers my past, I acknowledge it and sort out what was then and what is now. My husband's wounds also get triggered at times, and his reactions are similar. It can happen so quickly, and we can get lost in the shuffle of unresolved pain. Projecting all of it onto each other is not the answer. Instead, we must sort out our past from our present. It takes time, commitment, and honesty. Blaming one another keeps us stuck in our individual histories.

Over time I learned to better understand myself. I learned I must take time to truly understand who I am and how I am in my world. Sometimes I like what I see. Other times, I behave in ways that cause me pain or shame. The goal of self-reflection is not to beat ourselves up but to understand where we have been, where we are, and where we want to go. We must be compassionate and loving with ourselves. Sure, we can justify our words and behavior, but the goal is to treat ourselves with the same respect we would treat another. Blaming, scapegoating, and ghosting impedes our growth.

The hurt child within comes bursting out at times in an attempt to be seen, heard, and healed. Our inner child is often scared, fragile, and reactive. To help her to heal, we must treat her as we would another child, with tenderness, love, and compassion. We must learn ways to deal with conflict in constructive and healthy habits. As we heal our past, our inner child grows, and eventually, we are one. Tantrums cease, and increased communication and compassion help us release our past pain and heal in healthy ways.

Unresolved trauma will continue to impact ourselves and others until we process the issues in our past. Present relationships and situations can easily trigger our wounded selves, such as smells, sounds, people, places, or feelings. Emotions must be acknowledged, felt, and released, regardless of what caused the pain. It takes courage, commitment, and responsibility to grow and become healthy. The support of loved ones helps tremendously.

As we deal with our past, our cracks begin to fill. With loving, reliable support, we can process our hurts and let go of survival tactics which once served us well but now only negatively impact our present lives. Sometimes, medications can be effective in helping us to manage the after effects of trauma including insomnia, flashbacks, depression, or anxiety. However, over-medicating can impede our ability to help ourselves and heal. Finding balance is essential.

Sometimes we leak our emotions at inappropriate times. We react as opposed to responding. We may cry or rage at small things that, usually, we would have ignored. Leaks trigger reactions. It often happens unexpectedly and unconsciously. We can momentarily act out the pain within. Darcie Sims, a specialist in compassion fatigue, says we leak when we fail to care for ourselves. Leaking also occurs when we are taking on the pain and suffering of others. Absorbing too much emotional baggage day after day will inevitably cause us to leak and burn us out as well. We cannot heal or fix others. Only they, themselves, can. We cannot give more of ourselves than we need for ourselves.

Our body alerts us immediately when we are not okay. For example, headaches, fatigue, or stomachaches arise when stress arises. If ignored, serious health issues can develop. Being mindful of what our bodies communicate is necessary to deal, heal, grow, and release all that does not serve us.

Years ago, when I was in a treatment center, forgotten memories and intense emotions exploded into my consciousness, I felt physically and emotionally overwhelmed. The lack of full-blown memories, only scattered pieces, made it more difficult for me to process. Well-meaning clinicians re-traumatized me by probing too much into my past. The upsurge of trauma was so intense that it disabled me and disrupted my sleep for months. I felt terrified of everything and trusted no one.

Initially, I was overmedicated and misdiagnosed, which further disabled me. In time, the clinicians and myself began to understand what I needed to heal.

It was the scariest and most confusing time ever in my life. The disjointed puzzle pieces of images, feelings, memories, smells, and sounds escalated my fears. I realized my body would not have reacted like it was unless trauma occurred. I released the need to perfectly piece the puzzle together or try to make sense of it. I accepted the overwhelming and unbearable impact of my past. With appropriate professional and personal support, I learned to express my emotions and process the pain of my past.

Today, we understand trauma more thoroughly and understand how to help people heal in healthier ways. EMDR (Eye Movement Desensitization and Reprocessing) is one way and proved to be a lifesaver for me. There are many other treatment modalities that help us to heal in less traumatic ways. Equine-assisted therapy is another life-changing way. Tapping is another modality. Today, a variety of efficient and effective therapeutic programs are available to help us to recover and prevents us from being re-traumatized.

All of us have cracks. Some of us may possess deeper cracks than others. Regardless of size, cracks create dysfunction in our lives. Most of us have experienced harmful or neglectful experiences. Many of those may be repressed or buried until they are triggered. We struggle when we find ourselves in a crack. The consequences are the same, regardless of the depth of the crack. Most of us deal with feelings of unworthiness, guilt, and shame in our lives. All wounds require healing. In time, as we can heal our wounds and become whole. We may carry invisible scars, but that is okay. Learning to embrace all of who we are, the positive and the negative is essential to thoroughly understand ourselves. Scars remind us of how far we have come, our resilience, and where we want to go. We have come far. We need not carry pain, shame, and worthlessness for the rest our lives.

Cracks become the scars on which we build a solid foundation of integrity and urgency to live life in ways that are most meaningful, purposeful, and sacred.

CHAPTER 11

EVERYDAY WOUNDS

*"Our scars and wounds only heal when
we touch them with compassion."*
– Buddha

Not all of us have lived traumatic lives. Yet most of us have been wounded somewhere along the way. In life, unexpected events occur that profoundly impact us. Our unique experiences often pave the way toward living with greater purpose and meaning.

I've yet to meet a person who has not experienced pain at some point in their life. It could have been a death, divorce, illness, job loss, poverty, abuse, bullying, or something else on a long list of possibilities. Regardless of the incident, all of us will experience pain that pierces our hearts, causes our confidence to shatter, and impacts our lives forever more. Some of us may endure more than others, yet all of us experience pain that changes our world. These experiences are the spiritual lessons we agreed to before birth. These experiences help us to grow and become more.

Death has profoundly impacted my life. Family and friends died long before their time to illness, drugs, alcohol, suicide, or murder. Death reminds us that there is no guarantee of tomorrow. Death has so much to teach us. Pain and suffering challenge us to dig deep and find our resilience.

I lost two brothers. The first, Bozie, my 18-year-old twin, died suddenly. It was sudden and tragic finding him and trying to resuscitate him. Because he was my twin, others have thought his death was more challenging for me to recover from than the death of my second brother, David. David died following a ten-year illness. David's death proved more challenging for me because I witnessed his many complicated and horrific medical procedures. David experienced uncontrollable pain, medically induced paralysis, amputations, and more. There were many events I had to process and recover from, which took more time to process and heal, than my twin's sudden death. Sudden deaths often leave us with unfinished business and no time to say goodbye. Yet, all deaths challenge us in unique and personal ways.

There is a great difference between experiencing one tragedy versus many. Regardless of origin, chronic suffering requires more time to process and heal. Each life experience offers its challenges. A sudden life-altering event immediately shatters our sense of safety in our world. There is no time for goodbyes or closure. On the other hand, chronic traumatic events result in multiple wounds to our psyche and self-esteem. It's excruciating to be so powerless in the face of a loved one's suffering.

I do not yet know what it feels like to die, but I have been the loved one left behind. To feel so helpless and powerless in the face of loved one's suffering is very difficult. Medical procedures can be traumatizing to witness. The slow passing of the physical body before us is life-changing. Afterwards, it takes great resolve to honor how our loved ones lived as opposed to how they died. The duration and length of the experiences we witnessed impacts the time it may take to heal.

What matters most is how we perceive our experiences, not how others think we should. We are not them, and they are not us. We do not heal in the same way. We must be mindful that even those who love us may deny our reality because it triggers their unresolved issues. Those who reject our reality can unknowingly create more distress for us. Wounds are unique to each individual. Those of us who choose to heal will need to lean on the loving support of others until we can gain greater inner strength and confidence. Trying to convince those who deny our reality prolongs our suffering. When dealing with difficulties, we must honor ourselves and how we need to heal.

When I lost my twin brother, I was 18 years old. I had unhealthy coping skills, and learned to escape life through the use alcohol or drugs. Blaming myself for knowing no better only caused greater suffering. I had to find compassion for myself and accept that I did the best I could with what I knew at the time. I did not know healthy ways to cope and I survived the only way I knew how. Those around me were just as lost and had little to offer. I did the best I could at that time. I learned that blaming or shaming myself impedes my ability to heal and grow. I accepted who I was then. It took years of sobriety and therapy, but I now know better. Today, my choices are healthier. Traveling down a dark and dangerous road taught me what I did not want in my life. I learned to embrace my past, learn from my mistakes, and move forward in life. I do not choose to be bound to my past.

Growth starts from the inside out. We cannot improve the relationship we have with ourselves or others until we embrace all of who we are. It's difficult to acknowledge the pain I've caused myself and others. Our wounds do not dissolve on their own. Wounds remain dormant until they are triggered and erupt. When that occurs, we must take radical responsibility to heal our pasts. We can only create the lives we love when we honor and heal ourselves.

Because we are imperfect human beings, we will continue to make mistakes. We can strive to learn from our mistakes, find better ways to cope with life, and cease behaving in ways that cause us greater harm. We can forgive ourselves as we would another loved one. Demanding more from ourselves than we do from others drains us, just as unrealistic expectations set us up for failure. Beating ourselves up significantly harms us. We have many available options to assist us, such as coaching, therapy, 12-Step programs, and more. There is no excuse to harm ourselves or others.

We all have what we will ever need within us to heal our lives regardless of what we endured. We often learn more from pain and suffering than we do from joy and happiness. Wounds present opportunities to grow and develop. Difficulties propel us to dig deeper and live more meaningful lives. Life can make us bitter and angry, and blaming. But we can choose to become more. Comparing ourselves to others is a waste of time. Pain is pain, regardless of cause. Minimizing, justifying, or rationalizing our pain ceases our ability to grow. Life is God's gift to us. What we make of our lives is our gift to God."

If we commit to healing inner selves, our outer world will radically improve. To heal, we must deal with our issues. Committing to releasing the thoughts and actions that no longer serve us is necessary to become whole. Regardless of where we have been or what we have experienced, we can choose to move forward and embark on a positive and healthy lifetime journey.

Healing is a gift we give to ourselves and others. We must give voice to what was and let it go if we want to create a better future. We must take full responsibility for our words and actions because they can be weapons and significantly devastate and destroy ourselves and others.

My friend Michele gave me a beautiful pearl necklace by Bryan Anthony's, and the package insert shared the following words: "This is your life. Do what makes you happy. Change what you can and let go of what you can't. If there is something that you want, get it. If you have a dream, follow it. Do not let fear hold you back. Trust your instincts and believe in yourself. You are capable of more than you think. When people tell you that you can't, show them you can. There will be times when you fall, but you will stand again. Protect your heart, but recognize when to let go. Reminisce in the good times, but always look ahead. Learn from your mistakes, but do not dwell on them. Be confident in who you are, keep your head high, and remember you are beautiful. Don't be afraid to express how you feel. Cry hard, laugh harder, and when you love — love with everything you got. Never settle. Find your passion. You can be whoever you want to be. There are no set rules. There is only now. Now is the time. We have one life. Let's make it count." What a beautiful prescription for how to live our lives.

CHAPTER 12

RELATIONSHIPS

*"If your love for another person does not include
love for yourself, then your love is incomplete."*
– Shannon L. Adler

The most important and meaningful relationship we will ever have is with ourselves. How we perceive ourselves impacts everything we think and do, and the dreams we have for ourselves. Few people teach us about the importance of loving and honoring ourselves. So many of our negative thoughts about ourselves are unconscious, thus go unnoticed. Negative thoughts harm us in every way.

Early on, we learn about ourselves through the eyes and voices of those who care for us. Parents, caregivers, siblings, and teachers influence how we see, think, and feel about ourselves, positively or negatively. As children, we easily assume others' views of us as factual because we do not know any better. If the relationships with others are positive, we are fortunate. If the relations are unhealthy, our self-worth begins to crumble.

Unfortunately, many of us carry shame and struggle with self-worth issues. Caregivers can only take us as far as they have come themselves. If caregivers have poor self-esteem, it often gets passed down to the next generation. Until we take responsibility for changing the negative thoughts we entertain, they will continue to negatively impact us for the rest of our lives.

How we think and feel about ourselves often stays under the radar until it becomes problematic. It is essential to examine how we think and feel about ourselves. Unconscious, negative thoughts may swirl endlessly in our minds. We assume life is status quo because we do not know any better and we readily accept who others tell us we are and we do not often question the treatment of others.

When I was younger, the reoccurring theme in my mind was, "Please don't kill me." Although there was no evidence that others wanted to kill me, I felt unsafe. Fear, often unconsciously, dominated much of my life and sometimes still does. As a child, everyone and everything is larger and more powerful than children, which often exacerbates their fears. The unpredictability of domestic violence is overwhelming for children. Even today, I can easily feel threatened when people act out, even though I know I can keep myself safe. When others yell or raise their voice in anger, I automatically prepare to fight or escape. I often retreat into myself. Trust diminishes. I seek safety in my aloneness.

Trauma seems to be hard-wired into our brains. It takes significant work to examine, disassemble, and release what no longer serves us. Family dysfunction imprints itself upon our psyche and being. It is essential to understand the things we tell ourselves. What we say or think about ourselves is much more impactful than what others say and do. With thousands of thoughts floating throughout our brains daily, we can easily entertain the negative ones and focus only on them. Negative thoughts can expand and become all-consuming. Becoming conscious of our thoughts and self-talk is essential for healthy growth and development. Being mindful of what we tell ourselves and replacing our negative thoughts with positive ones is critical if we desire to create healthy and productive lives.

I was forty-two years old when I met my second and present husband. In and out of therapy for years, I erroneously thought much of the pain from my past was behind me. However, it wasn't until I got intimately involved with my second husband that I realized I did not fully trust men nor think they would stick around. I unconsciously viewed male relationships as temporary, even though several of my past relationships had lasted over eight years.

The relationship with my present husband triggered buried emotions from the loss of my twin brother twenty-four years earlier. I realized I hadn't opened my heart to anyone since my twin's death. It was just too painful. Loving feelings between my husband and I mimicked the closeness I felt with my twin. Although these deep feelings frightened me, I wanted love and intimacy. However, it was not as easy a process. I sabotaged myself and our relationship multiple times before I gathered the courage to walk through my fears. Running from my relationship would have been easier, but I wanted intimacy in my life. I grew tired of feeling alone and knew my husband was worth it and very trustworthy.

In my husband's past, pain and betrayal arose as well. Our relationship triggered his painful past. Prior to our relationship, he had been betrayed by an ex who had an affair with his friend and work associate. The wounds of his past also surfaced to be healed. When we feel safe in relationships, our buried emotions arise to be healed. We can deal with our pasts and release the pain or continue to run from it. My husband and I did not allow our pasts to rob us of the love, joy, and intimacy we deserved. It was difficult. Therapy assisted us in better understanding our histories and its impact upon our relationship. We chose a better future for ourselves. We learned to love ourselves and each other.

Further complicating our relationship issues were several others who tried to control and manipulate our lives. In therapy, we learned better ways to deal with toxic, harmful, controlling people. We learned to honor and protect ourselves. We established a very beneficial ten-minute rule to vent and share our emotions and struggles, but not allow outside issues overshadow our everyday lives. We learned to let go of what we could not control and to focus only on what we had power over. Our bond deepened and became stronger. Our lives improved because we refused to endlessly entertain drama or negativity in our lives.

What I learned through that struggle is that all good and solid relationships go through growing pains. Although struggles are not easy, we can become better despite them. Oftentimes the love of another can help us to learn to embrace and love ourselves. Not giving up is challenging, but worth it. We could not have gotten to where we are today had we not worked through those trying and difficult issues.

I also learned that we often love others like we want to be loved, which does not always speak to those we love. It is so important to learn and to understand what makes another feel heard, honored, and loved. Everyone does not feel love in the same way. If we fail to love another in the ways that touch them, they will not feel fully loved. We need to explore ways that make us feel loved. How do you feel loved? Is it through words, actions, one's presence, or more? I want to love my husband well and I learned to express my love for him in ways that touched his heart.

All relationships challenge us. We relate to many different people in our lives, including spouses, friends, parents, peers, children, and more. Relationships present growth opportunities. We must protect ourselves by being selective in determining who deserves our time and attention. We will sometimes encounter unhealthy relationships in our families or workplaces. In those relationships, it's essential to not give more to others than we need for ourselves. We cannot allow unhealthy or needy people to drain us. If we do, it can destroy us. When exhausted, we have nothing to offer ourselves or others. We must weigh the costs of our relationships. If the cost is too great, it is time to let it go.

Healthy relationships enable us to rewrite our past and create a better present. Unhealthy relationships drain us. If we work through complicated issues with another person in healthy ways, it often positively impacts our lives. Remaining in an unhealthy relationship impedes our growth and development. We sacrifice our self-worth.

Before we can dispel negative self-talk, we must be aware of it. Entertaining negativity in our minds always brings us down and hinders our growth. We can learn how to think positive and loving to ourselves. It takes practice but is well worth it. We must learn to forgive ourselves when we make mistakes and take responsibility for making amends. Humans are far from perfect. We all have a lot to learn. Developing and nurturing positive thoughts about ourselves is a learned skill. It's a journey with many ups and downs. However, we fully blossom when we create healthy relationship skills and surround ourselves with loving, caring, supportive others. Life need not be a solo journey. We can lean on one another as we learn to love ourselves.

All relationships teach us. We become better or worse because of them. Asking ourselves what does this relationship have to teach me is important, regardless if it is positive or negative. What is this relationship or issue trying to teach me? Relationships cause us to pause. We must take notice of how each relationship impact us. We must release those that impede our growth and take us further and further away from ourselves. Healthy, loving relationships fuel us to become more. Unhealthy ones drain our life energy.

I've ended relationships unhealthy relationships. I stayed with others that repeatedly pulled me down. I've feared healthy relationships because I unconsciously felt undeserving. Everyone we come in contact with impacts us and our lives. Identifying who fuels or drains us is essential. To love ourselves we cannot allow others to spew toxicity and negativity onto us.

Not all relationships deserve our time and attention. When interactions drain and pull us down, it is time to protect ourselves and create definitive boundaries with such people. Some relationships are abusive, neglectful, and dehumanizing. Some relationships produce fear and shame. We know when it's time to move on from a relationship. Yet we may make excuses as to why we should stay. We focus on the good and deny the bad. We often fear being alone. Abusers are very skilled and manipulative at convincing us of who they think we are. Remaining in negative relationships causes us and sometimes others significant harm. Toxic people are hazardous. Harmful people frequently care only about themselves. Those who want power and control over us are dangerous. Staying in such relationships will devastate our emotional, mental, spiritual, and physical selves.

Most days, if we sleep well, we awake with a full cup of energy. Quickly our children, families, work, errands, and the like, begin to consume the energy in our cups. Learning how to reserve enough energy for ourselves is key. We can learn to avoid giving our power away to those who do not deserve it. Draining and toxic people suck the life out of us, and then they go on their merry way. We may allow them to drain us. Draining people dump on others and rarely seek help. They can easily take all we have without a care. It is essential to be kind and empathetic to ourselves first. We can't give what we don't have. If we do not care and love ourselves, we will feel drained and empty. We can learn how to truly love, honor, and nurture ourselves as we would our children or another loved one. It's the only way to blossom into all we are born to be. It's our choice. We are worth it.

CHAPTER 13

CARING, EMPATHETIC PEOPLE

"The struggle of my life created empathy.
I could relate to the pain, abandonment,
and having people not love me."
— Oprah Winfrey

Because empaths know pain and suffering intimately, they are likelier to engage with unhealthy people out of a desire to help. Experiencing difficult emotions enables them to empathize with others easily. Often, they can be found offering another hurt person support.

It's a beautiful gift to be able to empathize and put yourself in another's shoes. Yet, empathetic people sometimes assume others are like them. Compassionate people must be cautious not to carry the emotions of others. Sometimes we want more for others than they do for themselves which always drains us. Caring people can easily be taken advantage of because they are often naive in believing others are like them. In addition, they tend to trust others and not question their motives.

I was thirty-nine years old, single, and very vulnerable when I met my first husband who I'll refer to as Noname. Before meeting him, I had been involved in two separate long-term relationships but was not interested in marriage. Noname was charming, attractive, and smart. He asked so many questions about what I wanted in a relationship, explored my dreams, and was seemed genuinely interested in me and my life. Effortlessly, he quickly slithered into the ideal partner by listening closely and becoming my ideal partner. He appeared to be perfect for me at that time. I easily fell in love with the person I thought he was.

We married within months, and rather quickly, unconsciously, my life began to deteriorate. We were together for less than a year, including the divorce. The last two months of our relationship was spent supporting my mother as she was dying. Two weeks after her death, Noname left me, and I never saw him again. We had temporarily moved to New Jersey to help care for my dying mom. It was a meaningful, yet difficult time to be so helpless in the face of a dying loved one. By the time Noname took off, I was left with minimal self-worth, great confusion, many unanswered questions, and tremendous grief. Noname's skillful, manipulative behavior devastated me. His repetitive lies caused me to question my thoughts, emotions, and actions. Given my history and education as a therapist, I could not believe I got involved with such a manipulative and dangerous individual. In the aftermath, I struggled to understand how I got involved with such a toxic, harmful person.

Before meeting Noname, I was lonely and vulnerable due to multiple life stressors. I struggled with some family drama, a management position I detested, and harbored a deep longing to move closer to the East coast. The year before meeting Noname, I ended an eight-year relationship and accepted a promotion as a social work director of a home health/hospice agency I previously worked at. I managed peers I worked with two years prior. Some of those peers had long employment histories with the agency and I suspect were unhappy with my promotion. Supervising social workers with my professional license on the line every day was not for me. Nor did I like confronting those who had previously been my peers. A few employees disregarded my clear work expectations and became a challenge to manage. I quickly learned that management was not for me.

Given my emotional fragility at that time, my dreams of moving to the East coast, and the additional work challenges I later understood how I got involved with a narcissist. Noname also wanted to move and voiced similar career goals which resulted in us moving to the coast and working together as live-in house guardians to seriously traumatized teens. We did that for four months until I received a call from my sister informing me that my mother was dying with metastatic lung cancer and had only months to live. However, even before the move, there were signs of trouble in our relationship that I seemingly excused, rationalized, and minimized.

It would take me months, if not years, to heal from the negative and disruptive impact of that short-term, life-altering relationship. I thoroughly examined it from all perspectives and began to understand how and why I got involved with such an emotionally harmful person. Although I forgave myself, I desperately needed to know how it happened to prevent it from reoccurring. My empathy for people, combined with Noname's sophisticated, manipulative skills, decayed my soul. Despite my childhood history and professional training as a licensed clinical social worker, I had no context in which to understand such self-centered behavior. Believing in the inherent good of others blinded me from seeing his dark and dangerous personality characteristics. Love blinded me from Noname's self-centeredness and his very sophisticated, manipulative behaviors.

Getting involved with such a calculated,

manipulative individual forced me become brutally honest with myself. I learned how to trust my inner gut feelings when things do not feel quite right or good. I learned that looking only for the good in others blinds me from their darker side. Picking myself up from that destructive relationship was difficult, challenging, and painful. I had to see and accept aspects of myself that I didn't care to. I learned to carefully evaluate all my relationships and the impact they had on me. The ones that caused me stress needed close examination. I learned to be compassionate, forgiving, and empathic with myself in order to heal and grow. I learned that beating myself up only needlessly prolongs my suffering. Processing my pain and grief was complicated. But I wanted to be free of carrying such heavy emotions into the rest of my relationships and life. I willingly to shook, rattled, and rolled to reach the other side. I told myself that Noname was not worth me giving up my desire for future healthy relationships. I knew I was a good person and that there were many others out there like me. Giving up would have been disastrous for me. Despite my relationship with such an unhealthy person, I was determined to seek healthier, loving relationships. The deep heartache and pain I experienced in that relationship with him was not worth me giving up on life or others. I learned a great deal about myself and others from that experience. People are not who they always project to be. In time, we are better able to sort out the truth from the lies. So many lessons in such a brief relationship.

So many factors contribute to our relationship

choices. Understanding how and why we engage with those we do is important and necessary to prevent us from repeating our past. Hurtful people are not worth us relinquishing our dreams. We can heal, recover, and move forward from unhealthy relationships. Learning from our mistakes helps us to make wiser decisions and create better futures. Forgiving ourselves and others frees us to live more meaningfully.

An empathetic heart is a gift and, at times, a burden. Kind, caring, well-meaning people can be naive in assuming others are like them. They often give others the benefit of the doubt. They quickly forgive and forget. Abusers use another's empathy, kindness, and decency to their sole advantage to get exactly what they want.

Kind people are frequently targeted by abusers, narcissists, sociopaths, and the like. Kind-hearted, compassionate people are easy targets because they do not suspect that others have selfish motives. Narcissists and sociopaths initially present as someone they are not. They are often charming and friendly. They easily mold themselves into what we may want them to be, but it's a facade. Their sophisticated skills to control, manipulate, and readily use others fuels their grandiose egos, goals, and agendas. They lack insight, remorse, and emotional maturity and are incapable of developing authentic relationships.

It's essential to understand harmful behaviors and personality traits which only harm us. Abusers, narcissists, and sociopaths rarely, if ever, assume responsibility for their behavior. They believe they are perfect, and the problem lies with the other person.

They blame others for their deplorable actions. They minimize our thoughts and emotions. They camouflage their intentions and come across as caring and considerate. They use our own words against us. The level of calculation these individuals exhibit is difficult to initially recognize. There is always a motive that serves them, not you. Their view of themselves is utter perfection. Thus, they do not like to be questioned or second guessed. Questions and confrontations frequently anger them because they truly believe it's you with the problem. Their words do not match their actions. Yet, they say all the right things and mostly that we want to hear.

Manipulative personality traits warrant our immediate attention because of their harmful, life-changing impact on others. Dangerous people not only lack remorse, but they are manipulative, exploitative, and frequently violate the rights of others. They exhibit power and knowledge which devastates and destroys others.

Unfortunately, we may encounter such people in our families, workplaces, and social groups. Until they are discovered, they are generally well-liked, charming and charismatic. They adore and need lots of attention and possess great showmanship. Subsequently, when issues later arise, we often blame ourselves. Narcissists are persistent in manipulating others to believe their lies while scapegoating us. They frequently minimize and deny another's thoughts and feelings. Challenging their inauthenticity sends them into a sudden rage which results in major conflict. They are all-knowing. They often succeed at isolating us from our loved ones. We become so torn down, we become easy pawns for them to further manipulate.

It takes tremendous courage, commitment, and support to end unhealthy relationships. Victims will often blame themselves until they understand the sophistication of their abusers' manipulative and deceptive skills to destroy their self-worth. There is no working through issues with self-centered people because their problems are always projected onto us.

When we have sufficiently distanced ourselves from harmful people and look in our rearview mirror, we will likely see the red flags we ignored. We realize we made excuses for their aberrant behavior. We justified their destructive behaviors. When a relationship shatters our self-esteem, it is a sure bet we were involved with an abuser, narcissist, or sociopath.

We can better protect ourselves from harm by paying close attention to how we feel in the presence of others. Initially, all is well, but it does not stay that way. As soon as we begin to second guess ourselves, it is a clear sign we are involved in a dangerous relationship. When our self-worth plummets, we are in trouble. We must be mindful and notice if one's words match their actions. Often their words and actions are incongruent. Tuning into ourselves and adhering to our ever-subtle inner messages is vital. Our gut reactions are the body's attempt to protect us. When fear or confusion arises, we must ask ourselves if there is an immediate threat, and if so, we must do whatever we can to keep ourselves safe.

Rebuilding our lives following toxic relationships is

challenging because our self-esteem is devastated. The longer we stay in harmful relationships, the longer it takes to process and heal. We possess the power within us to rise and shine in the aftermath of such hurtful relationships. Destructive relationships cause us to become wiser and more powerful. We cannot allow them to destroy our lives. Toxic people walk away leaving us swimming upstream. But the good news is, we can heal. We become better equipped at evaluating others because of what we endured.

Toxic people exist but we do not need to keep them in our lives. If they remain in our lives, we must develop clear and firm boundaries. Our job is to protect our integrity from their wrath. We limit our time and exposure to them. Or we can entirely eliminate them from our lives, if possible. Clearly understanding that to egotistical others, relationships are a manipulative game they often enjoy. Unaffected by any emotions, they continue to wreak havoc on anyone who crosses their paths. They love to be idolized. It is always all about them and what they want.

The better we arm ourselves against those who try to tear us down, the more we will live happier, healthier lives. We need not socialize or involve ourselves with anyone who does not support or love us well. We chose who we want in our lives and who does not deserve to be.

CHAPTER 14

MANAGING OUR
TIME AND ENERGY

*"Your time is limited, so don't waste
it living someone else's life."*
– Steve Jobs

Today, so many things can drain our energy and zap our joy. The things we allow to deplete us often go unnoticed. Technology, needy people, negative thoughts, and intense emotions are huge energy suckers if we allow them to be. Every day, if we rest well, we awake with a full cup of energy. Yet sometimes, by noon, many of us feel empty, without ever realizing who or what depleted our energy. Being mindful and aware of what fuels or drains our energy helps us to better manage ourselves and create healthy, happy lives.

Daily living responsibilities consume a great deal of energy. Raising children, cooking, cleaning, bathing, shopping, laundry, working, pet care, praying, meditating, reading, volunteering, hobbies, thoughts, emotions, and maintaining relationships consume so much of our time and energy. However, reserving energy for ourselves is essential if we want to live happy, authentic, balanced, and meaningful lives.

We cannot blame others if we fail to reserve energy for ourselves. Blame is often an excuse to shirk self-responsibility. It's vital to be mindful and fully aware of what depletes our energy. It is also necessary to refill our energy cups and need to identify what and who fills our reserves. Setting healthy boundaries with partners, children, bosses, friends, and foes is essential to maintain balance in our lives. We are equally as important as those we love. We must learn to care for ourselves as we do others. It's not selfish. It's a necessary requirement for healthy living.

As a former hospice social worker, I frequently felt depleted because I prioritized work over myself. The needs of others presided over mine. Dealing with life and death is unpredictable and often emergent, so it was easy to neglect myself and put work responsibilities before my own needs. But that didn't serve me. Rather, it often caused me to feel tired, drained, and depleted, which was my fault. I had to learn to preserve time and energy for myself. I came to understand that it was necessary to make time for people and things that gave back to me and filled my cup. I learned to be a better caregiver to myself and others when I made time for myself to do things I loved. It was a process that enabled me to examine and prioritize work and my needs. Both are pertinent to my health and well-being. I am more emotional and mentally available for others when I take the time to do things that restore me.

I also depleted my energy by trying to get to every sports game played by my three stepsons. I usually worked evening hours and would rush from work to games. Eventually I learned I could not have to attend every game without exhausting myself. I told my stepsons I could not make every game because work was challenging at times. I further shared that sometimes I needed time just to shake off the day and needed alone time to release work issues. I asked them to share the highlights of their game when they returned home. I struggled with feeling guilty, but as I continually reassured myself that I need time to care for myself. When I took the time to be alone and process, I was much more open and receptive to hearing about their day. When I failed to care for myself, I often felt drained and unable to be fully present for others. My family and I learned about the value of self-care and how it enhances your life. I encouraged my stepsons and husband to care for themselves in the same way.

Darcie Simms, an expert on compassion fatigue, offers valuable self-care wisdom through her workshops and writings. She's created excellent, eye-opening activities that help us identify how we leak energy, allow needed people to drain us, and, most importantly, how to develop healthier lifestyles. Learning how to preserve our energy is challenging, but vital if we desire to create meaningful and fulfilling lives. Consciously prioritizing our needs and those of others enables us to create lives we love. We are better for it. Our families function better as well.

My work experiences with hospice and trauma often drained me because I put the needs of others before my own. I functioned on empty, as many of us do when we do not prioritize our needs. Hospice work, like many other challenging jobs, sometimes exposes us to intensely draining life and/or death situations. It's meaningful work but also energy depleting. Learning to manage our personal and professional lives is necessary. Understanding what depletes us and what refuels us is important. Hospice work continually reminded me to live each and every moment because we do not know what tomorrow may bring. Just as I would encourage patients to live fully until they die, I had to also tell myself of the same. I could not give to others what I failed to give to myself.

Self-care must be a priority. Without it, we leaked and give all of our energy away through relationships, work, and other responsibilities. I grew very tired of being exhausted because of my own doing. When I began to say no to others, it was a yes to myself. Frequently feeling empty and continual suffering forced me to set needed boundaries at work and at home. Just because we can do things does not mean we have to.

All of us encounter personal and work experiences that demand and consume much of our energy. In trying times, we must become diligent and treat ourselves with equal kindness and compassion. We owe it to ourselves to do whatever is necessary to foster and nurture our own health and happiness. Filling our cups with joyful, happy, and meaningful moments further enables us to give to ourselves and others in healthier ways.

We cannot steal time. We must make and take time specifically for ourselves. Developing time management skills helps us to preserve the energy effectively and efficiently that is needed to pursue our personal passions and dreams. A simple perspective exercise is to jot down everything we do in a day. Then, look at the list and identify what we must do. Then, highlight the things we do not want to do. We could delegate and ask others to help with those tasks. Is what we want to do even on our lists? If not, why? Delegating responsibilities, carpooling, coordinating playtimes, setting boundaries, and avoiding draining people are but a few suggestions that can lessen our energy output. Yet, it doesn't stop there. Be sure to add the things that fill our cups and energize us. The things that we do that we love always give back to us. Without a healthy balance of give and take, we drift away from ourselves. We must clearly identify what and who fills our cup. We must make time for the people and things that regenerate us.

Giving all our time to our children, mates, employers, friends, and more prevents us from becoming all we are born to be. Feeling guilty is normal in the beginning. However, the more we create lives we love, the easier it becomes. Then, one day, we realize the guilt is gone. There is no need to feel guilty when we prioritize our needs. We teach others that we matter, too, just as they do. We demonstrate that self-care is a gift we give to ourselves and others. Honoring ourselves and taking time for ourselves is necessary and one of the greatest gift we offer to ourselves and others.

CHAPTER 15

BEFRIENDING
FEAR

Fear is a reaction. Courage is a decision.
– Winston Churchill

Throughout our lives, fear will arise, regardless if it is a mental perception or an actual threat. Fear is debilitating, paralyzing, and often freezes us in place. Fear impedes our hopes, dreams, and passions. Sometimes it's real, and sometimes it is self-imposed. The only way to release fear is to walk through it. Fear is the opposite of courage. When we walk through our fears, we gain courage and strength.

Fear dominated much of my life. Fear rooted in the cells of my body. I became hyper-vigilant, growing up in an unpredictable, domestically violent home. People scared me. When my father was enraged, he would smash glasses, dishes, and condiments against the floor or walls. The violence of his actions created tremendous fear within me. Our home was not a place where I sought peace. Nature and animals became my refuge.

Sadly, my parents carried a lot of unresolved issues and emotions from their past. At times, often when drinking, they were explosive and aggressive. I don't condone harmful behavior, but I've learned to understand it. So many factors contributed to my parents' painful, destructive behaviors. I sensed the depth of their unhappiness and brokenness. I know they loved me and tried to do their best with what they knew then. They, too, suffered grave realities as children.

Furthering the fear my twin and I experienced were the dramatic plays my older siblings would enact when babysitting us. My siblings were nine to sixteen years older than us. When caring for us, they sometimes created very creative, but dramatic scenes that terrified my twin and me. They played out scary scenes unaware of the fear they instilled. They enjoyed acting and entertaining their selves and played out dramatic scenes in our presence, such as a Martian going door to door in our neighborhood, looking for people to take or hurt. My brother would then go outside to stop the villain. There would be a lot of unseen commotion outside that my brother and I heard, but not see. My brother would run back into the house with a ketchup-stained, torn shirt, reporting he fought off the bad guy. Too young to understand such scenes were fake, we shook with fear. My siblings didn't realize the harm they caused. They were children acting out their own difficult emotions and issues through play.

When we were adults, one of my older sisters shared that she would have me pack my bags when I was very young. She told me no one loved me anymore and I had to go. Before I reached the top of the street, she would call me back, and I would desperately run into her arms. She said she did that because she wanted to feel loved. She was a hurt teen trying to find the love she needed. She found in a very inappropriate way to get her needs met.

I faintly remember these childhood experiences and wish my siblings had never shared them. I ache for the little girl I was then who didn't understand why those in my family hurt or scared us. I've always known that my siblings love us and we wholeheartedly love them. Our family has endured great pain, anguish, and loss over the years. Such behavior can easily happen when the pain and anger of children or adults, is repressed and not addressed, it gets acted out. I, too, am guilty of hurting others when I was angry and pained. I'm not proud of it. I learned to forgive myself and to do better. Unconsciously and sometimes unintentionally, we, too, hurt ourselves and others in attempts to deal with our repressed emotions or issues.

Gavin DeBecker, author of the Gift of Fear, writes, "Unwarranted fear will kill more people this year than violence." Unwarranted fear arises from our minds, the past, or what possibly could happen, but often does not. Unwarranted fear does not cause an immediate threat. In comparison, warranted fear occurs because there is an actual present threat.

How can we deal with fear? When fear arises, we must ask ourselves if there is a legitimate threat to us. If not, then it is self-created fear. We can acknowledge it, feel it, and let it go. We can talk to ourselves about how capable we are to keep ourselves safe. We let go of thoughts that escalate our fears. We acknowledge unwarranted fear, but we must not entertain such thoughts. Entertaining negative thoughts is dangerous and detrimental to our mental and physical health. We stress our bodies when we accept crazy, fearful thoughts as our reality. We cannot control what thoughts come into our minds, but we can negate them and replace them with more positive messages. Entertaining anxious thoughts unnecessarily escalates our anxiety and angst.

Redirecting our thoughts is a learned skill. Thoughts that flow into our minds do not control us. We can choose at any time to change them. We simply replace the negative thought with a positive one. It is a skill we can master if we consistently practice it. In time, we will learn to notice unhealthy thoughts, but not focus on them. We merely change our thoughts to positive ones and entertain those. We have full control over our minds.

Fear can quickly escalate to a point where it will mentally shut us down. When that happens, we struggle to sort out our present reality. Escalated fears can immobilize us physically, emotionally, and mentally. It is so important to remember to breathe in such times. Breathing calms ourselves in scary situations and enables us to think and function better. Fear causes tremendous stress in our bodies, minds, and souls. When we are fearful, our body tenses and tightens, our blood flow constricts, our hearts beat faster, and our thoughts get scattered and confused. When our thoughts restrict, we struggle to think clearly. We often react in ways we usually would not. Conscious deep breathing is a simple tool that lessens our angst and helps us to think more clearly. Breathe in to a count of four and breathe out to a count of four. Slow, conscious breathing helps us to calm our minds and bodies. We can then better control our thoughts and respond in more helpful ways.

My husband shared with me that he cannot tell when I am scared or upset because I always look okay on the outside. I know he loves me and supports me, so I seriously contemplated what he said. I do not try to appear okay when I am not, but in my past, I thought I had to in order to survive. Repressing and denying my thoughts and emotions was how I learned to survive in childhood. What I came to realize was just how much I betrayed myself in the process. I had to learn to communicate better when I am not okay because I deserve support when I'm struggling. What once was a helpful survival tool is no longer necessary in my marriage or other relationships.

Living in fear is a horrible way to live. We must find ways to release and process our fears, real or imagined. Meditation, exercise, yoga, breathing, prayer, playing, laughing, and replacing our fearful thoughts with positive ones are ways to lessen our anxiety. Differentiating between warranted and unwarranted fear is essential. Fear is an emotion we can learn to control and respond to in healthy and productive ways. It is our responsibility to create peaceful, nurturing lives devoid of unnecessary fear.

Sometimes, we are afraid of change, or becoming all, we can. We get very comfortable with our everyday routines which is often a safety net. Going outside the box, taking risks, ending relationships or jobs that do not serve us frightens many of us and can immobilize us. What would happen if we did go for it? What is the worst possible thing that could happen? Something better is waiting for us if we act? We can think our way into better living. We must take the necessary steps to create lives that fulfill us. But we must act. Thinking about living your dreams never makes them happen. We must take small, consistent steps to create lives we love.

Fearful thoughts stress in our bodies. Chronic stress can be fatal. Managing our thoughts enables us to make better choices. Entertaining only healthy, positive thoughts brings us closer to our goals. Creating beautiful lives happens when we act, taking one small step at a time.

Not very long ago, I was deeply hurt and angered by comments from the farm owners where I boarded my horse. Their harsh comments triggered great fear in me. At the time, due to safety concerns regarding my horse, I chose not to confront them. The hurtful and abusive comments triggered some buried feelings of fear and pain, which rose to the surface during the confrontation. It was my responsibility to feel my present thoughts and emotions and sort out those from my past. Confronting the farm owners would have escalated my fears. I worried about possible retaliation against my horse? As much as I desired to address abusive issues in that conversation, I knew it would have fallen on deaf ears. I realized who these people were and did not think it was worth my time. Their aim was to blame and hurt me. They succeeded at doing that. Sharing my thoughts or views would likely have resulted in an all-out confrontation that would have accomplished nothing. I heard them loud and clear. I was not wanted on their farm. I told them I would leave as soon as I could. I consciously chose not to battle with them because it would have created greater, unnecessary distress for me. The situation could have been dealt with in a peaceful humane way. I would have honored their wishes without the abuse. The situation could have been much different. I learned that people are not always who they seem to be. I learned to continue to honor myself and what I believe, despite the thoughts of others. I learned that some battles are not worth fighting.

Unhappy, fearful, and insecure people spew toxicity onto others. We must pay close attention to who we associate with and the impact of our relationships. There are too many people who live in fear. Not only do they live in fear, but it is further fueled by inundating themselves with the negativity on television and the web. All of our actions significantly impact our lives. If we inundate ourselves with negativity, we will be negative. If we surround ourselves with positive, optimistic people, we are more positive and hopeful. Examining the impact of one's words and actions is necessary. We need to pay attention to who supports or negates our dreams.

Faith also helps us to release our fears. Regardless of what or who we believe in, asking for divine help to dispel them is easy. We need not fight fear alone. Asking a higher power to free us from fear and grant us the courage to move through it lightens our load. Depending on only ourselves makes it more difficult. There is help available if we want it. Letting go and allowing our higher power to help us to do what we struggle to do for ourselves is easy.

Learning to overcome our greatest fears is necessary for personal health and growth. We can do this. Being mindful of ourselves, our interactions, and our responses is important. Fear and anxiety are clear messages conveyed through our bodies, informing us that something in our lives is not okay. Ignoring our fears take us further away from ourselves.

Asking questions such as, what just happened? Why am I not okay? What occurred that caused a change in my attitude or feelings? Was it a conversation or something else that contributed to my mood change, such as television, internet, or a phone call, etc.? Questions trigger us to examine the present and determine what impacted us. We must be diligent in examining our experiences because such information helps us to care for and protect ourselves.

Knowing how fear impacts our mind and body enables us to respond, as opposed to react, and make sound decisions. No one enjoys fear. It's a powerful and impactful emotion. Fear may present as dread, apprehension, anxiety, foreboding, fright, fury, or panic. If fear consumes us, we are less able to help ourselves. Befriending fear and walking through it is how we empower ourselves. It is often how we become more. Fear cannot control our lives. We have the power to deal with or dispel it, if we are willing.

Many of us are so far removed from ourselves that we struggle to identify our thoughts and emotions. We unconsciously disregard our own thoughts and feelings. We cease living in the moments of our day. We can befriend our thoughts and emotions and learn from them. Emotions aren't destructive. Emotions are normal. How we deal with our thoughts and emotions makes the difference. The choice is ours.

Verbalizing fears often disempowers them. Fear causes us to examine our lives. Sometimes, we fear what we can become more than what we do not. Becoming all, we can is scary and uncomfortable. But it is worth it. We must be daring and true to ourselves? We deserve to live free of anything that impedes us in all we possibly can. Let's go!

CHAPTER 16

PROBLEMS BEGIN
IN OUR MIND

"Your thoughts are the architect of your destiny."
– David O. McKay

Despite our best efforts, we will experience life challenges, big and small. Our minds have the power to inflate or deflate what impacts us. We cannot control the thoughts that float into our heads, but we can choose the thoughts we want to entertain. My friend, Justin Dunn, says that we can control our thoughts rather than our thoughts controlling us. We can release negative, harmful thoughts, which negatively impact our emotions and behavior.

Personalizing what others say and do frequently creates unnecessary problems for us. The closer the relationship, the greater the challenge to redirect our thoughts. All of us are sometimes guilty of personalizing the words or actions of others. It's so important to understand that the behavior of others is often about them, not us. We control how other's words or actions impact us. Not personalizing the words and actions of others enables us to process experiences in better ways. We often assume we know why others act the way they do, but often we are wrong. Understanding that the behavior of others is more about them, than us, helps us to process it in healthier ways.

In 1998, my mother died of metastatic lung cancer a few months after her diagnosis. Shortly before her death, when we were alone, my mom experienced a sudden burst of air hunger which caused her significant anxiety and panic. She struggled to breathe. She pulled at my clothes and pleaded for me to help her. She was suffocating. As previously instructed by her hospice nurse, I gave her liquid morphine orally in a syringe, which lessened her panic and allowed her to better breath. When I dispensed the morphine, some of it slid down her chin and onto her clothes. I gave her a little more. She relaxed and fell asleep. However, she never regained consciousness and died the next day. It was a horrifying experience for both of us.

Afterwards, I struggled with horrible thoughts about whether I hastened her death. Processing that harrowing experience took time. I knew the morphine I gave her did not take her life. If morphine had caused her death, she would have succumbed immediately. But at the time, I allowed those thoughts to control me. My inability to control my thoughts caused me greater pain and heartache.

What I learned from that experience was to thoroughly examine my thoughts and determine what was true from what was false. I didn't end my mother's life, but negative thoughts floated in my head. I entertained the negativity for a while until I learned better. I could continue to entertain those ugly, negative thoughts if I chose to. I realized the power I have over what thoughts I chose to think about. For example, I could look in the mirror, identify my flaws, and focus on them. I can assume everyone I see that day sees my flaws as well. I could take all interactions personally because I feel bad about myself. I could choose to unnecessarily hurt myself.

We sometimes entertain negativity without even realizing it. On good days we are positive and feel good about ourselves and others. On bad days, we destroy ourselves by entertaining negativity. We can begin to notice our thoughts, without reacting to them. We can let go of the negative ones. We possess the power to focus on only what we chose. Thoughts will never control us unless we allow them to.

In my previous hospice work, I witnessed many dying people. Drugs were provided to ensure a peaceful and pain-free death. Do prescribed medication help one to die peacefully, or does it hasten their death? I am not a doctor, physiologist, psychic, or pharmaceutical expert. I do not fully understand how and when a body begins to shut down. Even if I were an expert, my goal in assisting my mother that day was to decrease her suffering. My intent was not to kill my mother. As a dying person's body begins to shut down, there is less interaction with the outside world. I have seen this many, many times. Yet, I second-guessed what I knew to be true by entertaining the trash within my head. I believed I eased my mother's suffering, rather than hastening her death. I can only hope that if I begin to suffer at the end of my life, my loved ones will do the same for me.

On June 16th, 2020, I was diagnosed with stage IV incurable lung cancer, and surgery was not an option. Thankfully, immunotherapy was an option. My past work with hospice and my mother's air hunger incident exacerbated my thoughts and fears about death and dying. I witnessed many lung cancer deaths. However, I also found people who are presently living with stage IV lung cancer. I wanted to be in the latter group. Releasing my negative, fearful thoughts took time.

Following my diagnosis, I did not want to talk about my cancer. I couldn't. I felt very overwhelmed and frightened. I asked my oncologists to tell me what I could do to help myself, as opposed to focusing on the cancerous tumors in my body. I struggled but eventually gained better control over my thoughts and emotions. Thoughts of dying ceased swirling endlessly in my mind. I focused on living which enhanced the quality of my life. I focused on what I could control, such as diet, thoughts, and support, and began to eliminate anything toxic and stressful in my life. I quickly realized that I wanted to live more than ever before.

It takes tremendous effort, support, and prayer to manage thoughts in trying times. We need not entertain negative thoughts or allow them to control us. We must replace negative thoughts with positive ones to foster hope and life. It's easy to let our minds run away with unhealthy thoughts, which only hurts us. Healthy living requires us to discard all that does not serve us. Cancer taught me how to fully embrace my life and value my time. Cancer taught me to better love and care for myself. I thought I had good self-care skills, but realized I had so much more to learn. I frequently put others' needs before my own which was very harmful and possibly fatal.

Prioritizing life, healing, and positivity made a world of difference for me. I realized my diagnosis does not define me. It's only a tiny part of who I am. I am much more than a cancer patient. Despite any life challenge, we are capable of becoming more. We can and must focus on the good in life and practice gratitude. Discard all negative thoughts and replace them with life-affirming thoughts. It is our choice. We cannot control the thoughts that enter our minds, but we need not entertain them. Failing to control our thoughts harms us and creates tremendous suffering. There is no need to further hurt ourselves.

Our mind is a powerful tool. What we think, believe, and respond to impacts our feelings and lives. I was victim to my suffering for far too long. I allowed negative thoughts to linger, and caused myself needless suffering. I do not suffer well and grew very weary. Frightening, negative thoughts sometimes float into my mind, but I am much quicker to release what no longer serves me or enhances my life. Living with cancer reminds me to focus on creating a life I love.

I am far from perfect. I do unconsciously hurt myself at times. I've grown weary of draining people, places, and things. I learned to manage my life better or suffer the consequences. If life isn't working for us, why not try something different? We can stop beating our heads against the same wall. To live well, we must become willing to release all that doesn't serve us. We must commit ourselves to living the best lives we can. It is difficult to do when others spew negativity and pessimism onto us. Letting go of everyone and everything that drains our energy enables us to have the greater energy to create beautiful, loving lives.

I hope you never experience a severe, life-threatening illness. I hope you learn to love and care for yourself well. Diseases are complicated, draining, and time-consuming. Self-care and honoring ourselves is serious business. Time is sacred. Let's focus on what we want in our lives. Every time, we ignore our needs, we suffer. Cancer taught me so much about living and relationships. The cost of living in entertaining negativity is great and very damaging to our health and well-being.

Healthy living requires courage and hard work. It's easy to be happy when things are good. Challenges arise when life gets complicated. Negativity and toxicity will always create more pain and sorrow. The willingness to think and act positively is possible. We cannot allow negative thoughts, emotions, or people to drag us down. We deserve better.

People do their best with the knowledge and understanding they possess at the time. But, sometimes, it's just not enough. Living well is not for the weak and weary. Understanding ourselves and others takes tremendous work, but it's worth it. We must strive to create greater joy, peace, health, and happiness in our lives. Too many of us have sacrificed and neglected ourselves for far too long.

Some of us will not choose to better our lives for many reasons. Perhaps it's too difficult. Maybe it's easier to blame others. Many of us are guilty of wanting so much more for others than we do for ourselves. That is draining. We cannot control or change others. It's very painful to witness our loved one's struggle. No matter how much we want to, we cannot change others. We can only change ourselves, our thoughts, and our reactions.

Let's be responsible for creating and designing the lives we truly love. It takes tremendous commitment, effort, and courage to know ourselves, our wants, and what does not serve us. The path to enlightenment, happiness, and joy is ours if we so desire. Let's pull on our big girl or boy panties on and go for it.

Our happiness is our responsibility. We need to examine our thoughts, emotions, decisions, relationships, and more and ask ourselves what does or does not support our dreams. If something doesn't, what does it cost us? Are we willing to sacrifice ourselves as if we do not matter? We matter. Others are not the cause of our unhappiness. We are. We possess the power to control of our thoughts, emotions, attitudes, actions, and relationships. Let's begin to live every day as if it is our last.

CHAPTER 17

COURAGE

"Courage is not the absence of fear, but the triumph over it. The brave man is not he who does not feel afraid, but he who conquers that fear."
– Nelson Mandela

Webster's dictionary defines courage as the ability to conquer fear or despair. How do we conquer fear and pain? It begins by showing up for ourselves each and every day. We must learn to have our backs and understand we deserve to care for ourselves as we do for our loved ones. Asking God to help us to love ourselves, as he loves us, is an important step. Courageously loving ourselves is a life-long process.

We can learn to accept and love all of who we are. Loving ourselves is not selfish. Loving ourselves is the foundation of living well. Loving ourselves does not mean we are more worthy than others. It means we are equally as worthy. Courageously loving ourselves is not an event. It is a committed process that takes time to learn and practice. Courageously loving ourselves as God does is essential to becoming all we are born to be.

It would be awesome if learning how to love ourselves well was required in school. To love ourselves thoroughly we examine our lives like never before. Courageously accepting and understanding every facet of ourselves, the good and the not-so-good, is essential. Our experiences, personality, temperament, culture, race, gender, religion, and more, is very unique and valuable. We can begin to live true to ourselves by exploring our strengths, weaknesses, relationships, choices, dreams, and more. The journey to self-love requires great courage, commitment, and faith.

Fearing the judgment of others prevents us from moving forward. People often judge us when they are feel threatened or insecure. Judgers may criticize everything about us. But their judgments are more about them, than they are about us. Differences between individuals need not warrant an attack. Some people attack who and what they fear. We can and must learn to stand courageously in our truth without regret, apology, or argument. We are allowed to be who we are. We choose how we want to live. Living true to ourselves is a continual process throughout life. Accepting our gifts and brokenness helps us to heal, serve, and create lives that allow us to soar. Healing, forgiveness, and clarity help us to build a solid foundation, just one step at a time.

We need support and help from others to blossom. We must create support systems with people who love us well and are honest with us. We honor our vulnerabilities, forgive ourselves and others, and move forward. Allowing others to see our fragility is scary, risky, and challenging. Learning to lean on others when needed helps us to weave meaning, purpose, and intimacy into our relationships and lives. We must be daring and courageous to be seen if we want to thrive. If not, we often remain captive in our self-made prisons.

The courage to become all we are born to be is challenging because we change as we grow. Who we are at 20 years old is often very different from who we are at 30, 40, or 50. Experiences change us. Sometimes we change for the betterment of ourselves, and sometimes we get stuck.

Transformation and growth are challenging. It takes courage to stand firm in all of who we are, especially in the presence of hurtful others. Understanding and honoring ourselves moves us closer to our dreams.

Difficult experiences can fuel us to become more. We must ask ourselves what is the lesson we are to learn from a difficult experience. Our struggles are often our spiritual lessons.

We need not sacrifice ourselves for the sake of an unhealthy relationship. Relationships will challenge us at times. In healthy relationships, both parties choose to work through issues in respectful ways. We must ask what does this relationship cost me? Some relationships totally drain us and often cause tremendous heartache. Yet, we choose who and what we allow in our lives. Walking away from harmful others is necessary to create healthy lives.

If relationships do not foster our well-being, we move forward and release them. If not, they will continue to drag us down. The more we accept negativity and criticism, the greater our struggle. We are responsible for the choices we make, good or bad. Too often, we forfeit our needs for the sake of maintaining relationships. Yet, we deserve more. We must preserve energy to create lives we love and cherish. Lingering in suffering is martyr like and detrimental. We must summon our strength and integrity to become more. To live our dreams requires us to courageously triumph over fear one step at a time.

I previously wrote about a painful farm experience. Prior to that confrontation, I had been praying to connect with more like-minded people who share similar horsemanship philosophies. I moved two weeks after the farm incident. I moved to a farm where the humane treatment and love for horses flourished. I prayed for like-minded others, but do not know if I would have mustered the courage to move my horse because he seemed happy there, but I felt lonely and sad. I put my horse's needs before my own. It wasn't until after the move that I realized my prayers to connect with like-minded others was answered.

In retrospect, the confrontation led me to a better place. I moved to a private family farm that did not want boarders. However, when I told them I needed to move my horse, the new owners immediately began creating a beautiful space on their farm for me and my horse, Partner. They are very kind, giving, and spiritual people and wanted to help. They labored for weeks to create a space for us. They asked for nothing in return. I am very thankful for their generosity and kindness. God answered my prayer in an unexpected way. It was a trying time. Yet, the outcome surpassed my expectations. This is a perfect example of how God or a Higher Power works in our lives. Ask, and we shall receive. Our desires may come in unexpected ways. Yet, many of them do manifest. I am beyond grateful for the gracious, open-hearted, kind, loving people God placed in my life, whom I am blessed to call my friends.

Courage is about finding the strength to move toward our dreams. Courage is about walking through our struggles and caring for ourselves as we pursue our dreams. Courage requires us to trust in a power greater than ourselves and believe we are deserving. Courage is a choice. Living in fear prevents us from blossoming. God has surprised me many times in my life. I believe that God wants more for us than we do for ourselves.

Letting go and asking God to help us courageously create the lives we deserve requires faith in someone or something much greater than ourselves.

CHAPTER 18

TRUTH

"This above all: To thine own self be true."
– William Shakespeare

Shakespeare's words ring deep in my soul. They are so powerful. If we cannot be utterly truthful with ourselves, we cannot be honest with others. So often, we fail to see the lies we live. We unconsciously and repeatedly lie to ourselves, our families, our communities, and the world because we want to fit in. We try to belong at the cost of ourselves. Forfeiting ourselves disconnects us from God and others.

Truth is such a powerful word. Truth frightens us. We convince ourselves that the lives we have created are fine and we learn not to make waves. We often deny our truths to please others. But, what about ourselves? We often deny our needs for the sake of family, work, friends, and more. But what about ourselves? We may tell ourselves all is well. Yet inside, our pain, sadness, and anguish accumulate. When we forsake our truth, we distance ourselves, our families, our friends, and our divine selves. Occasional moments of clarity arise, but we feel powerless or immobilized to live lives we desire.

Opening ourselves to others when our thoughts, beliefs, and views differ is frightening and sometimes risky. Taking risks often triggers our vulnerabilities. Being vulnerable takes great courage. When we chose to share intimate pieces of ourselves, we can fear judgment and ridicule. Keeping peace is not worth forsaking ourselves. Do our loved ones genuinely support us in becoming all we are born to be? Do our family and friends encourage us growth, even it means a change for them? Not always, because our dreams may impact their lives, and many people chose comfort because they fear change.

Truth-telling has been a part of my life purpose. I realize truth often rattles people. Truth angers those who are unable to deal with it. Living true to ourselves is a road less traveled. Yet, the only sure way to create authentic, meaningful lives is to be very honest and forthright with ourselves and others. It is okay if our truth rattles our loved ones. If others love us well, they will support us. If not, we face opposition. Families, workplaces, learning institutions, and friends may want us to stay exactly where we are for their sake. That is conditional love which is never satisfying for us.

We must ask ourselves if we are genuinely happy with those we are involved with and how they impact our lives? We cannot allow the opinions of others to override ours. We must not sacrifice ourselves to make others happy? If we continue to disregard ourselves, we become more distant and resentful. We cannot blame others for what we fail to do for ourselves. Our life is our responsibility. Allowing others to direct our lives is detrimental in every way. Being nice cannot be more important than being honest with our selves? Many of us are guilty of doing this at times. Others cannot control us unless we allow it. Yet, some of us may never step up and claim our lives because they choose to do what others want them to do.

What do you know to be true for yourself? Do you have your own back? Are you creating a life of passion, meaning, and purpose? Are you merely go through the motions of life? What prevents you from living the life you love? It's easy to deny ourselves in order to belong in our families, communities, and organizations. We must embrace ourselves as we create the lives we love. If we do not, it is our fault.

While growing up, I denied the realities of my life. It was too painful to be honest with myself. That is how I survived. I found ways to escape the pain, and the lies I told myself. As a young adult, poor decisions led me further from myself. I was lost and unhappy much of the time. My relationships lacked intimacy. I was tired of suffering and running from myself. I was 31 years old, when my life completely fell apart. I could no longer tolerate living as I had been. It took tremendous work, time, prayer, and support to accept who I was and what I wanted in my life. It has become a lifelong process.

When I fell apart, it was a struggle to feel whole. I had to let go of friends who continued to escape their lives in unhealthy ways. I needed time to heal and release what no longer served me. I betrayed myself for far too long. I took one step at a time. There were times I was too afraid to live but more afraid of dying. Moments were sometimes all I could handle. I was emotionally, mentally, and spiritually broken and could no longer run from myself. I prayed to God and hoped I would arrive at a better place. Strength came when I needed it the most. In time, my life became more manageable, and I began to build a meaningful life. Doing the things I didn't like helped me to figure out what I did. I began to be honor myself and embrace how far I've come.

I have no regrets about how I lived or the mistakes I made. I learned a lot from my past and my pain. In recovery, I found people who genuinely cared about loved me until I could love myself. I began to feel hopeful about my future. I learned to let go and let God. I began to understand that my loved ones did the best they could with what they knew at the time. I also owned the hurt I caused myself and others.

Taking an honest inventory of our lives is difficult. We need to understand how we got there. We need to learn better ways to care for ourselves and others. We need to examine our relationships, decisions, and more. We need to continually check in with ourselves to determine if we are being true to ourselves. Our answers are within. Owning who we are and what we want is how we begin to truthfully embrace our lives. The lessons we learn from our difficulties enable us to assist others in the future.

I know God is not responsible for our heartache or problems. We are skilled at doing that for ourselves. However, God does utilize our struggles in order to help others. God helps us to find the silver lining in our difficulties. Challenges force us to grow stronger and wiser. Our suffering need not be in vain. We are here to learn spiritual lessons and to share our wisdom.

How does one begin to be true to oneself? It starts by thoroughly examining where we are in our lives today. It is important to understand how we got here and why. We release everything that doesn't support us, regardless if it is a job, person, place, or something else. When we let go of what doesn't serve us, we begin to create lives we love. In owning our truths, we are able to blossom and grow into all we are born to be.

CHAPTER 19

INTEGRITY

*"A true leader has the confidence to stand alone, the
courage to make tough decisions, and the compassion
to listen to the needs of others. He does not set out
to be a leader, but becomes one by the equality of his
actions and the integrity of his intent."*
– Douglas MacArthur

Integrity. How do we begin to create a life with integrity? What does integrity mean? How much of our lives do we own? Are we willing to take sole responsibility for creating and designing the lives we love? Are we able to take risks, big or small, and sometimes fail, yet pick ourselves up again when something doesn't work out the way we wanted? Creating a life of integrity requires us to fully embrace ourselves and make daily conscious decisions that foster love, respect, compassion, peace, health, and much more.

The real testament to a life well-lived is how we forge through tragedy, difficulty, disappointment, vulnerability, pain, and anguish, and learn all we can from it. When life is good, it is easy to flow with it. But when life is challenging, it can be devastating, demanding, draining, and piercing. Giving up or quitting is a choice. We can pull ourselves up and walk through the muck, knowing this too shall pass, and find the silver linings, or we can give up. The choice is always ours.

It takes courage, persistence, and tenacity to overcome challenges. It often causes us to shake, rattle, and roll to reach the other side. It is worth it. Having the courage to own our thoughts, emotions, and attitudes, and acting is how we become more. We are willing to release all that no longer serves us. Our struggles are testaments to ourselves and others. We lead by example and can be role models for others to do the same. Our struggles or spiritual lessons guide us toward meaningful living. They enable us to thoroughly understand what is important, as well as what is not.

Who do we idolize? Why do we emulate how they live their lives? All idols experienced great difficulty or tragedy but choose to stand firm in their integrity. My idols are Mother Theresa and Princess Diana. Both endured great struggles. The impact of their lives touched many. There are so many people to admire, such as Gandhi, Martin Luther King Jr., and so on. Idols triumphed over adversity and became more because of their experiences.

Integrity is built upon our choices, decisions, and actions. Our decisions either enable or disable us from creating sound, beautiful lives. How others react to our choices is none of our business. Our decisions, if in accord with our values, will lead us to greater joy, fulfillment, and purpose. We can learn from every lesson, relationship, and situation if we remain open to what the experience offers. Nothing happens by mistake. Consciously and consistently evaluating where we are, what we want, and what we need helps us create lives of integrity. We can grow through our experiences when we remain open to what it is trying to teach us.

Forsaking ourselves, denying our dreams, or living in the shadow of others prevents us from forging a life of integrity. We cannot blame and resent others for what we fail to do for ourselves. We cannot continue to neglect our wants and desires if we are serious about living true to ourselves. Living with integrity is a life well lived and worth it. It requires serious contemplation and commitment.

Idols have often risked, failed, and succeeded. Yet, they did not give up. They continued to pursue meaning, purpose, service, and love in their lives. They learned from their mistakes and continued to live with clarity. They were not defined by their failures. Their struggles became the mortar with which to build their lives. Our substance is determined by how we manage and respond to challenges.

One of my idols, Mother Theresa, lived with tremendous strength, integrity, resilience, perseverance, service, love, humility, and fearlessness. She lived a well-lived life. Mother Theresa epitomized compassion for all. She financially had very little but was beyond powerful. Her life made a massive difference in the lives of others. She embodied selflessness, compassion, and service.

My mother is another idol of mine. She was far from perfect, but her strength, faith, and hope prevailed through the tremendous tragedies she endured. My mom touched many lives in her lifetime. She turned her tragedies into compassionate service. She helped many people and made a valuable difference in the lives of others. I am blessed she was my mother.

Integrity can be the bedrock of our lives if we desire. Integrity requires us to examine our lives continually and to make conscious decisions that enhance our character. Integrity fuels us to rise above heart-wrenching experiences. We will fail, make mistakes, and even hurt ourselves and others at times. But we cannot give up. It's not what happens to us that is most important but how we deal with our experiences. Living with great integrity is indeed a road less traveled. We likely will be judged, ridiculed, and despised because others want what we have but are unwilling to do the work it takes to get there.

Unfortunately, there are many unhappy and insecure people living among us. Often, they inflict chaos and pain on others. I've been a victim of their misery. But we must not allow them to pull us down. Rather they can be the fuel that propels us to become more. We can live with integrity, despite them. We must focus on the people in our lives who love, support, and encourage us. We need not dwell on the hurtful actions of others. Becoming angry and bitter prevents us from achieving our goals. Hurtful and toxic others are not worth our time and energy. Despite broken others, we can thrive and survive. There is always good to be found in our world if we choose to look for it. Being grateful and thankful helps us to remain optimistic.

We need not to compare ourselves to others. Every one of us has a unique purpose. We all have gifts to offer. You can't be me, and I can't be you. Our divine gifts assist others in furthering their spiritual paths.

I could not have achieved much in life without faith. Believing in something greater than ourselves is needed in difficult times. Without faith, we flounder and fall. Our answers are within us. We embody divinity. The wisdom within us guides us to create meaningful and purposeful lives. Spirituality is very personal to each of us. We can and must connect with a power greater than ourselves to lead us toward our dreams. We agreed to come to earth to learn spiritual lessons. Our gifts enhance other's lives. We are divine beings.

I hope and pray that in sharing some of my life

lessons and what I've learned inspires you to become more and to love and honor yourself well. I pray you discover your purpose and freely share your gifts. I pray you learn to trust your inner wisdom and allow it to guide you. I want to continue to learn from my life experiences. I want to reap the benefits of your gifts. Life is ours and we can do whatever we wish to with it. May your healing and transformations bring you deep peace, love, joy, health, meaning, and purpose now and forever. God bless.

CHAPTER 20

HEALING AND
TRANSFORMATION

"We can't wait until life isn't hard anymore
before we decide to be happy."
– Nightbirde, Jane Marczewski

Healing enables us to become whole and healthy. When we live with greater awareness and health, our lives beautifully transform mentally, emotionally, physically, and spiritually. Growing, learning from our experiences, and sharing our gifts enables us to live with love, integrity, truth, and acceptance.

How do we transform our lives? In what ways can we grow and blossom? Are we willing to heal and become more? Transforming our lives often challenges us, breaks us, triggers tremendous emotions, and so much more. The transformational path radically changes our lives for the better. Healing motivates us to examine our physical, mental, emotional, and spiritual selves in all our stark nakedness. Healing transforms all of who we are.

Growing up in a dysfunctional and domestically violent home certainly pierced and damaged me in many ways. My siblings talk about fun times, and I wish I could remember happy times. But I have few happy memories from my childhood. There were good times, but the violence and abuse I witnessed overshadowed my joyful experiences.

At a young age, I started smoking and drinking alcohol. Drug use followed shortly thereafter. Substances enabled me to escape the pain and trauma. My parents escaped through alcohol, gambling and more.

My teenage years were a blur. I'm grateful I survived, given my frequent life-risking behavior. My twin brother died at 18 years old. Prior to his death, I lost several friends who were also making poor decisions. I was lost for years following my twin's death. I put myself in many risky situations that easily could have cost me my life. Yet I'm here. I believe I am a miracle.

When I was 22 years old, I ceased abusing drugs. However, I continued to drink excessively at times. I didn't know how to live without alcohol. I voluntarily entered an inpatient treatment center at 31-year-old. Once sober my life feel apart. A flood of horrific memories surfaced and caused serious problems I needed to work through.

Since that time, I've attended thousands of 12-Step meetings. I've sought help in therapeutic modalities, such as individual, group, EMDR, empty-chair, EFT, and reiki, and more. In sobriety, I obtained my Master's Degree, had several long-term relationships, and slowly began to rebuild my life.

In recovery, I buried my 45-year-old brother and other family members. I supported my sister, who had a massive, permanently disabling stroke. I buried my broken, abusive father due to Alzheimer's \and my mom to lung cancer. I married, divorced, and married a second time. I helped raise three stepsons.

I suffered significantly by the actions of dysfunctional others as well as by my own doing. I suffered for far too long. Thoughts of dying sometimes comforted me, but I feared death would be worse. Yet through it all, I knew God was present and would help me when I was willing. I was angry at God for some time. I blamed him, cursed him, and bargained with him, but somehow, I never lost my faith. If I gave up, I knew that those who had hurt me would have won. I was beyond determined to not let that happen. I worked hard to heal and become more. With each step forward, I gained greater faith and hope.

I grew sick and tired of wasting time and energy focusing on hurtful, negative others. I erroneously thought if I could understand the why they hurt me, I could keep myself safe. I eventually began to understand that I can keep myself safe, regardless of others. Life breaks us at times and causes us to dig deeper and become more. I know God does not cause bad things to happen. Rather, God utilizes our difficulties to enable us to transform and become stronger and more resilient. Believing in something greater than ourselves allows us to thrive and not merely survive.

The famous saying, what doesn't kill us makes us stronger, is true. But we must be willing to embrace the pain. We must move forward toward hope. We must believe we deserve better. Healing and transformation occur when we are willing to let go and let God, or whatever higher faith we believe in, to intervene and guide us to better living. I know no any other way.

To become as willing as a child and trust in something greater than ourselves supports us in healing and transforming our lives. In surrendering ourselves and our lives, we find grace, humility, and healing. Life becomes more meaningful. In doing so, I began to understand how my past was utilized to help others. I began to realize my pain and suffering was not in vain.

Challenging life experiences make us stronger. Regardless of what we endure, healing is not only possible, but necessary. We possess the power to heal and transform our lives in miraculous ways. As we heal, we learn to love and trust in ourselves, and a higher power to see us through challenges and become all we are born to be.

Who we are before challenges is very different than who we become after them. Enduring the unimaginable often propels us to create more meaningful and purposeful lives. We can survive and thrive, despite difficulties. If we follow our divine inner wisdom, we will create greater health and wellness.

Harboring bitterness brings more of it into our lives. Anger, pain, and resentment creeps deeply into our bodies, creating dis-ease, disease, and suffering. Our body houses our history, the good and the bad. Running from ourselves and failing to process our issues negatively impacts our mind, body, and soul. Our body always alerts us when we are not okay. Yet, we frequently fail to heed its warnings. We ignore headaches, body pains, and discomfort. We rationalize our symptoms and tell ourselves it will get better. We become sicker and more broken when we fail to listen to our bodies. Escaping from ourselves zaps our energy and prevents us growing.

Comparing our pain to others is useless and often an excuse to not deal with it. What we resist will continue to persist in our lives. Stuck in our muck-making stagnates and disempowers us. The result is we become helpless victims. But we are not victims. We can change our lives anytime we so choose. We can arise and become more despite what life throws at us. Learning healthier coping skills enables us to create better relationships with ourselves and others. Releasing all that does not serve us is vital.

Healing is possible, powerful, and transformational. Embracing all of who we are and living our lives in a way that work for us is a less traveled road. Many people will not do what it takes to get there. Transformation is a lifetime commitment which often entails many ups and downs. Challenges force us to dig deep, release what is holding us back and soar. Working through challenges helps us to blossom and live fully. Know we can rely on something greater than ourselves to guides and help us. We are but a small part in a grand universe.

Many people refuse to live to their full potential because of the work it requires. It's easier to be miserable. It's more challenging to create happy lives. It's the conscious decisions we make every day. If what we are doing works for us, that's great. But, if we are unhappy, struggling, and suffering, there is another way. Others, including our loved ones, may try to keep us exactly where we are because it benefits them. But we do not have to stay there. We soar when we chose to be true to ourselves and live with greater peace and happiness.

We also must be careful not to work harder at others' lives than they do themselves because it drains us and creates resentment. We can love others but must allow them to suffer the consequences of their decisions. We cannot do for them what they will not do for themselves. It's painful to watch our loved one's struggle. But their difficulties are their lessons to learn. We have our own lessons to bear.

Change occurs when we grow tired of suffering. We then become willing to change because we exhausted ourselves doing the same thing over and over again, and getting the same results. We must believe we have the power to change our lives. When others suffer enough, they, too, will change their lives.

Healing and transformation are choices. We are here to learn our life lessons. Our lessons enable us to grow and blossom. We need not suffer throughout our lives. If we do, it is because we chose to. It's not anyone's fault but our own. Healing and transformation happen when we let go and let God. Living well is a commitment we make to ourselves because we are worth it. We deserve to create lives we love and cherish. We must continually strive toward all that brings us joy, what makes us feel loved, and whatever makes us happy, peaceful, and fulfilled.

CHAPTER 21

CARING FOR
OURSELVES

*"Self-care means giving the world the best of
you instead of what is left of you."
– Katie Reed*

I've spent too much time hurting and suffering over the years. I've sought many healing modalities to help me to flourish. I've learned to embrace all of who I am. Caring for ourselves is one of the greatest gifts we can give ourselves.

Caring for ourselves is a full-time job and a huge responsibility. We can learn to love ourselves well, just as we love our children, partner, friends, and others. Committing to creating a life of health, peace, joy, happiness, and safety requires that we listen to our inner guidance and wisdom. We must take time to be alone with ourselves, without distraction. For it is in the quiet that we truly come to know who and what we are.

Understanding ourselves and the life we desire requires us to be present in the moments of our day. We need to stop doing and learn to BE with ourselves. Being alone with ourselves can be frightening if we avoided ourselves and now feel combustible, much like a shook-up can of soda ready to explode. We may want to blame work, family, friends, or whatever for where we are. Yet, it is our fault if we continue to deny ourselves, our passions, and our dreams.

It takes great courage to embrace our emotions, especially when they have accumulated. Faith helps us to know we can survive. Repressing our emotions creates greater struggles for us because now our feelings may be more intense and frightening. Phrases such as "I have a heaviness on my chest; My heart aches; I feel broken." These words capture intense emotion. The words describe how our emotions impact your physical beings when we embrace them. Feelings are powerful and normal. Emotions impacts us mentally and physically.

When I feel intensely emotional, I often turn inward in meditation, prayer, and silence. In silent contemplation, I know I am safe and God is with me. I do better when I let go and allow God to help me. Focusing on what-ifs escalates anxiety and creates greater confusion and stress. In the arms of God, I know all is well. Connecting with a power beyond ourselves brings greater peace and strength.

Letting go of negative and disturbing thoughts is a choice. I struggle like everyone else. I sometimes still try to control things I cannot. I unnecessarily exhaust myself. Endlessly doing the same thing repeatedly and expecting different results is insanity at its best. Learning to let go and listen to the wisdom within helps us to better care for ourselves.

Since my cancer diagnosis, I had to learn who and what depletes me and my energy. Because my disease lessened my energy level, I knew I must preserve some energy to do the things I love. My horse and nature give back to me in healthy, joyful, and peaceful ways. Both remind me to slow down and be present in the moments of my life. I've devoted so much of my life to caring for others. After my life-threatening diagnosis, I learned to put myself first and rid myself of unnecessary stress. Letting go and allowing others to care for themselves remains essential for my health. I know life is short. I cannot waste time on negative things, such as complaining, arguing, fussing, disagreeing, or draining people. Establishing and maintaining healthier boundaries enables me to better love, care, and protect myself.

Boundaries protect us, keep us safe, and help us to preserve mental and emotional health. Savoring and safeguarding our sacred time is how we maintain balance in life. Daily, I ask myself questions as if it were the last day of my life. What do I want to do? What brings me joy? How much time do I need to devote to tasks, appointments, work, and play? If this were my last day, with whom do I want to share my time? Boundaries are necessary to create lives with meaning, passion, and purpose.

I read a beautiful piece on Facebook that perfectly depicts the importance of decision-making. It stated, "You'll know you've made the right decision when there is peace in your heart. Stop listening to what the world says you should do. Start listening to your own heart. Only a few people in this world will stay completely true to you, and YOU should be one of them. Listen to your voice. Listen to your soul. Too many people listen to the noise of the world instead of themselves. Deep inside, you know what you want. Let no one decide that for you." How beautifully simple but profound.

Loving ourselves and healing are intertwined. We cannot have one without the other. We cannot heal if we do not care about ourselves. We cannot create a life we love and value if we do not take time to connect and understand ourselves. Why do we continuously struggle with self-care? We must take responsibility for ourselves and the life we choose to live. If we live in chaos, we choose that. Likewise, when we live in peace, we created that. The choice is always ours. We cannot blame others when we fail to care for ourselves.

In order to grow, we must cease doing the things that deplete us. We need to get out of our way and heed our inner wisdom. All of our answers are within us. Let's not beat ourselves up because of where we've been, the mistakes we made or our present circumstances. Let's accept that we have done the best we could with what we knew at the time and move on. Let's learn from our past, forgive ourselves, and live with greater grace, humility, dignity, and conscious intention.

Life is what we make it. Let's begin with giving ourselves permission to genuinely love and care for ourselves, as our creator does. Let's allow our inner guidance to lead the way. True transformation blossoms when we let go and allow God to guide us.

EPILOGUE

Upon finishing this book, life threw me a curveball in the beginning of August, 2021. I am tired, broken, helpless, and scared. I am struggling because my sister, who went on vacation to see her grandchildren, is in a New Jersey intensive care unit diagnosed with COVID. Mimi, her nickname, who is a very high-risk medical patient, is hospitalized, and I pray she pulls through. She has endured significant medical issues in the past twenty-seven years. At age 52, she suffered a massive stroke which instantly and permanently changed her life. The stroke left her with right-side paresis, blindness on the right sides of both eyes, expressive aphasia, and a deep and unshakeable sense of gratitude and faith. The year following her stroke, she endured nonstop seizures and has since remained on a ton of medication to keep them at bay. In the last ten years, she has been dealing with Non-Hodgkin's lymphoma, which resulted in multiple surgeries, radiation, and in the past year, endured intense chemo treatments. She became symptomatic with COVID a few days ago, despite receiving COVID vaccines.

I share my present pain, fear, and anguish aloud because it lessens the intensity of my emotions. Acknowledging it also makes room for good to enter my life. I have no control over my sister's life or death, but I need to process my intense emotions. I don't want my sister to die. Nor does she want to die. Negative thoughts and what-ifs render me useless. Insomnia, anxiety, fear, and negative thinking stress me and my health.

Life challenges us mentally, emotionally, physically, and spiritually. The choices we make during struggles helps or hinders our ability to cope. Tragedy has touched my life too many times. Although my difficulties made me stronger, I am tired. I cannot control what happens in life, but I can control response to it. I remain grounded and connected when I turn it over to God.

We maintain emotional stability by keeping life simple. Being honest with ourselves and fearlessly embracing our emotions in difficult times is essential to mental health. Ask ourselves questions such as, "What do I need to help manage this crisis? How can I take care of myself? Failing to care for ourselves creates greater suffering and upheaval in our lives and results in having nothing left to offer.

Every day, people face dire life situations. Some are much worse than others. Blaming others or escaping through addictive behaviors hurts us further. Owning our helplessness and powerlessness enables us to gather the strength to see us through. Believing in a power greater than ourselves offers us hope.

As I pray for my sister, I also pray for myself. I pray for the strength to be supportive, positive, and hopeful. Faith helps me to let go and let God control the things I cannot control. Surrendering is all I know to do. I listen to the wisdom within for guidance.

It's August 10th, 2021, and my sister Gloria and I are waiting to see Mimi's beautiful face to appear on a FaceTime call from the hospital. As she comes into view, we see she is peaceful, comfortable, and pain free. Mimi is no longer attached to breathing tubes, needles, pain, and more. Mimi's nurse gently and lovingly holds her hand. A nearby priest prays at the window of her room.

On the wall and ledge beside her are dozens of pictures of family and friends who love her. She is now free and communes with those who passed before her.

My beautiful, funny, strong, and loving sister, who physically endured so much in her lifetime, is gone. COVID protocols prevented her loved ones from being present with her. So many beautiful pictures of my sister's family and friends adorned her room. Loved ones prayed with Mimi prior to her death and gave her permission to go. Her body was devastated by COVID. Her history of lymphoma, strokes, heart disease, and more destroyed her health.

Several days before my sister's death, we talked on FaceTime, and she said through a tightly fitted oxygen mask, "Sis, I'm okay. I am going to get better. You will see. Life could be worse." In utter amazement and awe I thought to myself, how she could say such things when she could barely breathe. Her will to live was so strong, but her body gave out. Mimi was beyond positive, faithful, grateful, and thankful throughout her life. She never once forgot that others were far worse than herself.

Within hours of Mimi's death, I sensed her beautiful spirit and knew she was whole again. Her spirit was happy, light, and loving. Her loving spirit danced with joy and assured me she was happy and whole and doing okay. Her beautiful soul is now alive and well among us.

Death and dying is complicated. Challenges arise both for the ill person and those who love them. Both feel frightened, drained, and challenged. We must preserve energy for ourselves in trying times. Self-neglect drains us. When drained, we have nothing to offer anyone, least of all ourselves. Our decisions impact our mental, emotional, and physical well-being.

I've written about life purpose, divine wisdom, wounds and scars, anger, addictions, relationships, challenges, and more. I've shared some of my most heart-wrenching experiences to help you believe that healing is possible, regardless of circumstances. I've highlighted the importance of forgiveness, integrity, courage, truth, healing, transformation, and self-care. We can heal and transform our lives into whatever we want. Begin to fight fear with your faith. Cease making excuses. Let go of the past, live in the present, and plan for the future. Let's remember to control our thoughts and not allow them to control us. More importantly, act, take one step at a time toward greater health and happiness. Forgive those who hurt us and lets forgive ourselves. Release all that no longer serves us.

The tools we learn enables us to deal with difficulties, heal, and transform our lives. Our answers lie within. In sharing my heart and experiences with you, I hope you begin to create the life of your dreams. Create the life you love just one step at a time. Challenges will arise, but we can learn from them.

Mostly, I miss Mimi's voice, her laugh, her love, and her playfulness. For years, she often telephoned to check in. Never once did she end any conversations without saying I love you. Her passion, joy, laughter, and light remain. I wish I could hug, kiss, and thank her in person for all the beautiful ways she enhanced my life. Her life impacted so many.

Mimi did not fear death. She told my sister, Gloria,

that she was going to heaven when she died. Gloria asked how she knew, and she responded very assuredly that she just knew. Mimi never doubted God's deep-abiding love for her. She forgave quickly and knew God forgave her. Her faith was strong, solid, and lifelong.

Mimi's funeral was loving, intimate, and heartbreaking. She was deeply loved by many and often let them know what they meant to her. I didn't realize how much she enhanced my life. But her impact on my life was tremendous. In eulogizing her life, I share, "Mimi, I miss you every day. I miss your beautiful heart, love, support, sisterhood, and presence. You are one of the strongest people I have ever known. You never complained about your inability to see, walk, talk, or struggle. Your gratefulness and grace touched so many. Your legacy is one of love, laughter, play, and sincere appreciation of life. Your love was deep, affectionate, and lasting. Thank you for sharing your love, laughter, and light. Thank you for sharing your everlasting faith with me. Although I miss you, I know you are with us in spirit. Your crazy and fun-loving ways forever brighten our lives and make us laugh. Thank you for being my sister. Run free, my sweet sister, until we meet again."

I shared my sister's journey because she lived fully and true to herself. Daily, she told others how much they meant to her. She loved to play, laugh, enjoy, and enhance the lives of others. When illness stole some of her of sight, speech, mobility, and cognitive skills, Mimi continued to love and find joy in life. She was very grateful for what she had and lived with grace. My sister released her pain and easily forgave herself and others. She knew who she was and didn't apologize for being herself. Her legacy of living life to the fullest was evident to all who knew her.

My sister, like all of us, was not perfect. She focused on the positive in life and made the most of every day. She smiled often and found the simple pleasures of life. She was a perfect example of how to live authentically and joyfully.

The famous quote, "To thine own self, be true," is necessary in life. Lets live each day as if it's our last, doing what we love with those who love us well. We must know what brings us joy, peace, love, and happiness. We must know how to feed our soul. Jane Marczewski, Nightbirde's beautiful quote, deserves repeating, "We can't wait until life isn't hard anymore before we decide to be happy." We can be the change we wish to see in the world. OH YES, WE CAN!!!

Resources and Chapter Quotes

De Becker, Gavin. The Gift of Fear: Survival Signals That Protect Us from Violence, Dell Publishing Company, 2010.

Hay, Louise, You Can Heal Your Life, Hay House, Inc., California, 1999.

Sims, Darcie, Ph.D, certified thanatologist, a certified pastor, bereavement specialist, and a licensed psychotherapist and hypnotherapist. She was the president and co-founder of GRIEF, Inc.

Williamson, Marianne, Illuminata: A Return to Prayer, Riverhead Books, New York, 1994.

Chapter Quotes:

"Hurt children, wounds unhealed, too often become very dangerous adults."
Illuminata by Marianne Williamson

"If we stop distracting, we will stop destroying."
Soulshaping: A Journey of Self-Creation by Jeff Brown

"Our tragedies are our academies."
On Combat: The Psychology and Physiology of Deadly Conflict in War and in Peace Audio CD – Unabridged, November 12, 2013
By Lieutenant Colonel Dave Grossman

"Faith and fear both demand you believe in something you cannot see. You choose." – Bob Proctor

"Forgive others, not because they deserve forgiveness, but because you deserve peace."
The Five-Second Rule by Mel Robbins

"Happiness cannot be traveled to, owned, earned, worn, or consumed. Happiness is the spiritual experience of living every minute with love, grace, and gratitude."
Seeds of Greatness: The Ten-Part Formula That Unlocks the Power You Were Born With by Denis Waitley and Nightingale-Conant

"The body keeps the score."
The Body Keeps the Score: Brain, Mind, and Body in the Healing of Trauma
By Bessel van der Kolk M.D.

"To be angry is to revenge the faults of others on ourselves."
By Alexander Pope

"I came. I came to. I came to believe"
I Came to Believe by Alcoholics Anonymous

"It's easy to look at people and make quick judgments about their present and past, but you'd be amazed at the pain and tears a single smile hides. What a person shows is only one tiny facet of an iceberg hidden from sight. And more often than not, it's lined with cracks and scars that go all the way to the soul."
Sherrilyn Kenyon

"Our scars and wounds only heal when we touch them with compassion."
Teachings of the Buddha
Jack Kornfield

"If your love for another person does not include love for yourself, then your love is incomplete." – Shannon L. Adler

"The struggle of my life created empathy. I could relate to the pain, abandonment, and having people not love me."
Oprah Winfrey

"Your time is limited, so don't waste it living someone else's life."
Steve Jobs: The Life, Lessons & Rules for Success

Fear is a reaction. Courage is a decision. – Winston Churchill

"Your thoughts are the architect of your destiny." – David O. McKay

"Courage is not the absence of fear, but the triumph over it. The brave man is not he who does not feel afraid, but he who conquers that fear."
Long Walk to Freedom: The Autobiography of Nelson Mandela Mandela

This above all: To thine own self be true.
William Shakespeare

"A true leader has the confidence to stand alone, the courage to make tough decisions, and the compassion to listen to the needs of others. He does not set out to be a leader, but becomes one by the equality of his actions and the integrity of his intent."
Douglas MacArthur

"We can't wait until life isn't hard anymore before we decide to be happy."
Nightbirde, Jane Marczewski, an American singer and songwriter featured on YouTube, America's Got Talent, June 9, 2021.

"Self-care means giving the world the best of you instead of what is left of you." – Katie Reed

About the Author

Kathy Kehoe is a retired licensed clinical social worker, teacher, writer, group facilitator, and presenter. She has decades of experience in assisting others to heal and embrace all of who they are. She specialized in hospice/death and dying, critical incidents, trauma, abuse, and more.

Kathy can be contacted by email at kathy.kehoe10@gmail.com.

Made in the USA
Middletown, DE
21 January 2023

22141566R00106